Modern Religion
&
The Destruction of
Spiritual Capacity

The Gentle Wind Series

THE PSYCHOLOGY OF SPIRITUAL GROWTH

MODERN RELIGION & THE DESTRUCTION
OF SPIRITUAL CAPACITY

MODERN EDUCATION:
ONE SIZE FITS ALL

Modern Religion

&

The Destruction of Spiritual Capacity

Channelled from the Brotherhood
by Mary E. Carreiro

A Gentle Wind Book
Volume II

Bergin & Garvey Publishers, Inc.
Massachusetts

First published in 1988 by
Bergin & Garvey Publishers, Inc.
670 Amherst Road
South Hadley, Massachusetts 01075

Copyright © 1988 by Bergin & Garvey Publishers, Inc.
All rights reserved. No part of this publication may be reproduced or
transmitted in any form or by any means, electronic or mechanical,
including photocopy, recording or any information storage or retrieval
system, without permission in writing from the publisher.

89   987654321

Manufactured in the United States of America.

Library of Congress Cataloging-in-Publication Data

Carreiro, Mary Elizabeth
    Modern religion & the destruction of spiritual capacity.

    "A Gentle Wind book volume II"
    1. Gentle Wind Retreat (Organization : Maine)
2. Brotherhood (Brothers and Sisters of the Inner
World) 3. Religion—Controversial literature.
4. Spiritual life. I. Brotherhood (Brothers and
Sisters of the Inner World) II. Title. III. Title:
Modern religion and the destruction of spiritual
capacity.
BP605.G44C36   1988   291   87-24251
ISBN 0-89789-140-6 (alk. paper)
ISBN 0-89789-141-4 (pbk. : alk. paper)

RELIGION: from *religare* (Latin);
to tie back, to tie up, to tie fast.

—*Webster's International Dictionary*

Contents

A Prayer to the Logos

I pray that I am able to look
  at myself as I am every day,
That I might learn all that I can
  about my own negative patterns,
And that I might live long enough
  to make the necessary corrections.

This prayer should be recited each day by people who believe that this book—or any other book written with the intention of helping people—is too negative. These are the people who want light and love but are not willing to walk through the fire to find it.

Introduction

THIS IS A book about slavery. During the 1830s and 1840s, people in the United States began to speak out against human bondage. People began to see that no man or woman had the right to own another. At first, some people resisted the idea of freeing the slaves. They resisted because they had established comfortable lives that were based on maintaining slavery, and they did not want to sacrifice that comfort even for the sake of doing the right thing. Some resisted so strongly they were willing to fight a war in order to remain comfortable. However, when the ravages of war became more inconvenient than freeing the slaves, human bondage in Western society began to disappear.

This book is about spiritual bondage and the control of people's resources through religions. Religions control most of the available human resources on the planet today. They control these resources

---

*This book was written during the Spring and Summer of 1986, prior to the exposé of television evangelists in the United States. Though what is included here was not a reaction to those events, it will serve as an explanation.

by lying to people and preying upon their damages through fear and guilt. This is a much more serious kind of slavery than the kind that led to the Civil War. Religions enslave souls for thousands of years through misinformation about the world and life. Religions have caused people to believe in the fantasy of personal salvation and to ignore the reality of individual evolution. Religions have led people to invest in illusions about God and heaven and hell. Religions have robbed people of their purpose for living and turned them against themselves in a way that now breeds cancer and other serious physical problems.

At first, most people will resist the idea of freeing the souls enslaved by religion. They will resist because they have established comfortable lives built on the idea of personal salvation. Since personal salvation means that people do not have to do anything to be saved except "practice" their religions, people will not want to be inconvenienced by the reality of individual evolution. They do not want to face the hard work that is necessary to accomplish spiritual growth.

The information contained in this book was received from the Brotherhood through telepathic communication. The Brotherhood is a group of souls, both men and women, who are dedicated to the spiritual growth of humanity. This book, and the other volumes in this series, represent an aspect of an evolutionary project called Gentle Wind. However, publishing these books is not what the Brotherhood has come here to do. The Brotherhood has come to help humanity return to a path of evolution. This book will not, in and of itself, help anyone to evolve. It is not a Bible of any kind, nor can it save anyone's soul. It is not even a book about spiritual evolution.

It is a book about decontamination. Humanity is completely entangled in the damage and misinformation of a long period of spiritual darkness. It is as though the souls on this planet were once walking along a clear path and took a wrong turn into a huge briarpatch. Now, they are lost and entangled in the briars. They cannot go on with their journey because they are caught in these dangerous bushes. The more they wriggle and attempt to move, the more lacerated and torn they become.

This book is more like a technical manual describing the briars. It does not even give people the clippers to cut themselves free, because most people do not yet know they are caught in the briars. It is only meant to start a process of decontamination that for some souls will take hundreds and even thousands of years. For these souls, even reading this book over and over again will not begin to decontaminate them.

Over the past several years the Brotherhood has used Gentle Wind Retreat as a distribution center for information and for a healing technology that would make spiritual growth a genuine possibility. During this time thousands of people have received healing instruments, along with personalized evolutionary information called soul readings. Of the thousands who have participated in this project to date, only a handful of people have actually caught on to the reality of spiritual evolution.

The major cause of this failure to reach humanity can be found in religion and, in particular, in the idea of personal salvation. Personal salvation means that people are already saved by virtue of being born a Jew, baptized a Catholic, or by practicing a particular religion. Because people are already "saved," they do not have to do anything in order to grow. They can remain drugged on religious cliches. They can lead passive, comfortable lives because their eternal reward is guaranteed.

Nothing could be further from the truth. However, this fantasy of personal salvation is so sacred and so precious to humanity that people will do anything to protect it. It is a fantasy that is constructed out of lifetimes of religious endarkenment, and it is held in one form or another by over ninety-five percent of the people on this planet, whether they are currently practicing a religion or not. This idea is so well protected that people use most of their available resources to preserve it, leaving them with no energy to undertake the hard work of individual evolution. Herein lies the bondage.

Humanity can only be freed from spiritual bondage through the recognition of that bondage. This book was written so that people could begin to understand, in some small way, the spiritual devastation that religions have caused. You, as the reader, must determine the accuracy of this information. You must decide whether the televangelists are serving humanity or not. You must decide whether your priests, ministers and rabbis are healing people or not. You must decide who is telling the truth and who is living in fantasy. If you are not prepared to make these decisions, then do not waste your time reading this book. It will only make you unnecessarily angry and upset.

The Brotherhood has come to help humanity return to a path of spiritual growth. However, people only want growth if it does not interfere with their ideas of personal salvation. They want evolution as long as it does not challenge their personal comfort and spiritual passivity. People prefer the human way, which is always in conflict with the spiritual way. All the Brotherhood can do at this time is help humanity to see the limitations and difficulties of the human way. Since humanity created its own mental prisons and constructed its own spiritual chains and bonds, only humanity can free itself. Unfortunately, most people do not even know that they have been enslaved.

1

RELIGION
vs. REALITY

EACH RELIGION IN existence today has its roots in the era of darkness known as Kali Yuga. Kali Yuga (the Age of Darkness) was a
period of almost 75,000 years. During this time spiritual growth
on this planet nearly ceased. Accurate information about the nature and purpose of life was completely lost. As a result, people
have forgotten why they are here and what happens to them when
they die. People do not know what to do with their lives. Only a
few find any lasting satisfaction, no matter how successful their
lives seem to be.

During the centuries of darkness, people naturally sought answers to their questions about life and death on this planet. Out
of ignorance, fear, and the need to control others, religions arose
and attempted to answer these essential questions. Some religions
offered organized teachings and doctrines. Others offered simple
and primitive rituals. All were born out of human ideas and human
fantasies that have nothing to do with the actual reality of spiritual
evolution.

Religions are not without a purpose. In a time of darkness, religions keep the idea of God alive. However, any institution that is founded in darkness is born out of the human world rather than the spiritual world. Religions have kept the idea of God alive, but they have also developed extremely distorted and damaging ideas about spirituality. These distortions are all products of the human world and human fantasy that have nothing to do with spiritual reality.

Now the era of darkness is over. The Brotherhood, a group of spiritually evolved souls in the nonphysical world, has come forth to help humanity return to a path of purpose and meaning. They come for no other reason than to provide humanity with spiritual aid. They are here again, in this time of light, to offer accurate spiritual information and a healing technology to people who have the ability and willingness to return to lives dedicated to spiritual growth.

However, the Brotherhood finds humanity so damaged and misinformed by both religions and formal education, that very few people are actually able and willing to listen to their work. Religions have filled people with illusions and fantasies about God, Jesus, heaven, hell, and about personal salvation. People have come to believe they are already saved or that they can be saved, rather than seeing that they must save themselves through the hard work of evolution. Since people are already "saved," they have become spiritually passive and have completely stopped growing spiritually. Since they are already "saved," they do not believe that they have to do anything about themselves. They are free to run their lives on religious fantasies; to damage and hurt one another; and to do anything they want to the world in which they live.

Because people have substituted the fantasy of personal salvation for the reality of evolution, they have no room for accurate spiritual information. They are only interested in evolution as long as it does not interfere with their "pet" ideas about salvation. They do not want these fantasies challenged because they do not want to experience the discomfort of realistically looking at themselves and what they are doing with their lives.

Many people think they have not been influenced by religions or that they have broken from these influences. Yet, it is estimated that ninety-five percent of the people on this planet base their lives on the illusion of salvation. The New Age enlightenment seekers who look for swamis and gurus are all functioning with the same illusion. They are looking for salvation, only they call it enlightenment. Some of these people are the most burdened of all. They attend varieties of New Age workshops and seminars, consult psychics and psychotherapists, and add more and more trash to their already destroyed mental systems.

The Brotherhood finds humanity crippled by religious fantasies. People are paralyzed by religious misinformation to such an extent that it is simply not possible for the Brotherhood to work with humanity in the way that was planned. The Brotherhood offers this book, and others in this series, to those who can suspend their religious fantasies long enough to glimpse reality. Very few will actually be able to do so. People are so caught in the unconsciousness and automaticity of the human world that they have no room for accurate spiritual information. They are so filled with religions that do not provide any relief that they have no room for a healing technology that does.

THE HUMAN WAY vs. THE SPIRITUAL WAY

When a child is born, even to the most well-meaning parents, those parents have normal human ideas and expectations for that child. Normal children spend their early years attempting to meet the ideas and expectations of their parents. These ideas and expectations have nothing to do with what would be natural or correct for the child. Often the parental ideas are a product of the parents' damage or some compensation for damage done to the parents in the past. Nonetheless, all normal children attempt to fulfill their parents' ideas and expectations even though attempting to do so often causes the children personal pain and stress.

As the child grows up, the pain of living and behaving in ways that are both unnatural and incorrect causes that child or adult to rebel. In the initial act of rebellion there is often a feeling of relief. But relief is very temporary because soon the person feels guilty. When the guilt becomes painful enough, it drives the person back into attempting to fulfill the parents' original ideas and expectations. Then the cycle begins all over again. The person attempts to do something that is wrong for him. Life becomes painful. He or she rebels against the painful ideas and expectations. Then guilt takes over and forces the person back again to the parental ideas and expectations.

This is the human way. Every human being on this planet, living a life directed by the human ego, lives in these polarities. No matter how free or independent people claim to be, they are automatic, unconscious victims of this human condition as long as they are living a life directed by the human ego.

People all over the world suffer much mental-emotional upset because they are living unnatural, incorrect lives. Many people know that what they are doing is incorrect for them, but they cannot find a way out of the cycle. They are looking for peace but do not know how genuine peace is accomplished.

There is a spiritual way here—a way that the Brotherhood offers humanity. The spiritual way can only be accomplished through one's own individual soul. Each person on this planet came here to fulfill a specific purpose or destiny. That purpose is unique to each individual soul. Under ideal conditions, a soul comes to this planet in order to learn and to grow spiritually. Souls incarnate many, many times. Under ideal conditions, each soul would attract the situations necessary to fulfill its purpose and the individual requirements for spiritual evolution. Each consecutive lifetime would provide the circumstances necessary for the next step in spiritual growth.

In order for evolution to occur, the soul must first be connected to the human ego. Through this connection the soul can guide and direct the human ego to fulfill the spiritual needs of the individual soul. When the soul is directing a person's life, the person will no longer be bound to the cycle of the human way. The soul can direct the person to relationships and life situations that are both satisfying and spiritually beneficial. Unfortunately, the Age of Darkness has caused a great chasm to exist between the human ego and the soul. People are unable to connect to their souls—the only part of them that can direct the way to what is both natural and correct. Human egos are fulfilling their own human goals without any regard for their souls. People are preoccupied with looking glamourous, gaining power and prestige, getting attention for having the right car, clothes, marriage partner or house. They are living in hell while they claim to be seeking heaven. They cannot see that the more power they gain, the more they seek. The more money they make, the more they want. The human ego is never satisfied and therefore can never provide peace. The soul is dedicated to fulfillment and real satisfaction, but not through "success" in the human world.

Religions claim to offer peace. Religions claim to offer a spiritual way and a connection to one's soul. This is a lie. Religions offer very disturbed, distorted human ways. They offer human pain, pathology and misunderstandings that have caused humanity many serious emotional and spiritual problems.

For people to connect to their souls, the human ego must be repaired and quieted enough to resume its natural function as servant to the soul. Religions have not provided humanity with any such healing or repair. People have not been healed of anything by reciting a prayer or attending a weekly service. They go into their churches and temples with marital problems, parenting problems, mental illness, chronic physical pain, worry, fear, hurt, anger and loneliness. They leave their churches and temples with all their problems still in place. Not only have they been unable to find any real relief, but they have also become more burdened with the damages caused by the pathology inherent in the religion itself.

Religion is the human way and cannot provide humanity with a spiritual solution. People could imagine the presumed function of religion as a kind of hospital where people go for both mental-emotional as well as spiritual repair. They come to the hospital injured and damaged by life on this planet. They expect to find a competent medical staff and a hospital complete with all the latest diagnostic and treatment technology. They come as spiritual emergencies in great need of care.

However, instead of receiving proper treatment and real care, they are met by their religious leaders (who are pretending to be physicians) who say, "There is beige paint on the walls of Room 106." At first, people are shocked and confused. They have come to the hospital as emergency room patients in need of medical specialists, X-rays, oxygen, blood tests, medicine, and all available diagnostic and treatment procedures. Instead, they are told something so meaningless—"There is beige paint on the walls of Room 106." Over and over again the people hear these meaningless words. Soon, they become so mesmerized by the meaningless words they forget that they came to the hospital in search of relief. The words are like drugs that cause people to become unconscious about the pain, hurt, and suffering for which they were originally seeking relief.

All over the world people attend or have attended religious rituals full of meaningless religious cliches. They come in pain and in need of help. Instead, they are told, "Glory be to Jesus," "Praise be the Lord," "There is beige paint on the walls of Room 106." None of their pain is alleviated and their lives are not improved. They are drugged on meaningless religious cliches so that none of them remember the real pain and discomfort. They are neutralized by religious phrases so that no one will see the lie about religions helping people.

THE FOUNDATIONS OF RELIGION

Religions are not only born out of the darkness of the human world, they are also founded on ideas that have no basis in truth. Epistemology is the study of how someone arrives at the truth about something. Religious leaders all face great epistemological dilemmas because they cannot afford to look at how they arrived at their conclusions about life. If they examined how they came to their conclusions about the world, and about spiritual reality, they would see that their systems are built on very feeble, primitive thinking. They would know that these systems could not withstand an epistemological scrutiny.

For example, Christian ministers have come to the conclusion that the truth about life lies in the text of the Bible. But who decided that the Bible contained the truth about anything? Who proclaimed that the Bible could provide anyone with spiritual assistance?

The Bible is a collection of essays and stories. It has been declared a sacred religious work by massive agreement, not by overwhelming evidence. The fact that millions of people agree that the Bible contains the "Word of God" does not make that belief a reality. For the most part, the stories and essays in the Bible were not even written by first-hand observers. Nearly all of the Apostles, for instance, could not read or write. Their I.Q.'s ranged from sixty to seventy, qualifying them as retarded by today's standards of measurement. Their dictated accounts of what they thought they saw and felt were recorded by other people. By the time these accounts were written, they amounted to nothing more than hearsay. Hearsay is not even admissible evidence in a court of law, where people are trying to determine the truth. Yet, people have concluded that hearsay evidence is more than enough to formulate a spiritual guidebook.

Even if Jesus had actually written parts of the Bible, his writings would not have been coherent or necessarily sensible. When people quoted him, they were quoting a man who was living with extreme internal pressure. People cannot imagine the kind of continuous pressure that someone like Jesus would actually have been experiencing. His writings would have been aberrant, bordering on insanity at times, due to the pressure created by what he was attempting to do spiritually. Even if people had quoted him accurately—which was usually not the case—Jesus would not necessarily have made much sense.

The Christian ministers say that the Bible is the inspired word of God, but how do they know this is true? They say that their own sermons are also inspired, yet many of their sermons are senseless ravings that cannot help anyone grow spiritually. Are these useless ravings their idea of something that is inspired? The people who wrote the essays and stories contained in the Bible intended for them to be individual accounts of events that they felt were significant, not necessarily spiritual. However, people now agree that these stories are something that they were never meant to be. When people receive comfort from reading the Bible, it is not because the stories are comforting. Ninety-nine percent of the people who read the Bible are motivated out of loneliness. The writings remind them of times in their lives when they felt safe, either in church or simply surrounded by other people. The biblical passages themselves are not comforting. But the memories of being with people in church, rather than being alone, are comforting. People use the Bible to warm themselves when they feel cold and lonely inside.

If religious leaders took the time to examine how people reached the conclusion that the Bible was meant to be a spiritual guidebook, they would see that the history of the Bible is a history of false conclusions. For instance, people have also concluded that Jesus died to save humanity. In fact, his death had nothing to do with saving humanity. Jesus was simply trying to tell a few people, his followers at the time, about the individual hard work required in order for spiritual evolution to be accomplished. The essays in the Bible about his life contain none of this information.

The same thing is true about Moses, Muhammad, and other great men and women who have been written about in the various religious Bibles. Biblical teachings of all religions are based on false conclusions. When people set up their lives on false conclusions, they must then use their resources to protect their false realities, rather than using these resources to discover reality.

Imagine asking twelve schoolchildren to write essays describing the Challenger spaceshuttle disaster. Then imagine that someone found these twelve essays a thousand years after the Challenger disaster and compiled them into a book. Then the book would be sold and distributed throughout the world as though it contained the absolute truth about the Challenger tragedy, without question or doubt.

Spiritual growth is the only real reason for being alive, regardless of all the human fantasies about the purpose of life. People have blindly accepted various religious Bibles as though they contained the truth about spiritual reality, without question or doubt. Intelligent people accept the Bible even though it is based on faulty, infantile ideas. This thinking is extremely illogical and simpleminded. It is as though people decided that since ducks float and wood floats, ducks must equal wood. This would mean that when a person builds a house, he can always nail a few ducks together if he runs out of wood, achieving the same results. Once people use this kind of thinking, they then construct their lives so that no one can ever show them that ducks do not equal wood.

Religious leaders know that their information is feeble. They also understand that people will not attack infantile information, in the same way they would not attack a retarded child. Religious leaders capitalize on this natural vulnerability in the human consciousness. Religious leaders say ludicrous, absurd things all the time, but their sermons are so infantile that no one attacks them. People do not want to be seen as religious child molestors, which is how the human ego sees itself when it confronts anything that is innately weak and fragile.

Spiritual evolution is like building a bridge. To build a bridge, you would want a very elaborate, detailed, precise set of plans. Now imagine that you have been given a copy of a Bible—of any Bible—and asked to build a bridge from the text of this Bible. You know the information in the Bible is not what you need to build the bridge. Your priest, minister, or rabbi tells you not to worry, but to have faith; that by having faith, you will be able to build a safe, sturdy bridge from the information contained in that Bible. Obviously, if you accept this false reality you will eventually die without a bridge, and without ever learning how to actually build one.

This analogy is exactly what it is like for the soul. The soul has a mission to accomplish. It needs a very precise, detailed set of plans. In fact, evolution is difficult even with perfect plans. Yet, religious leaders give souls the Bible and tell them that this book contains all the information that they need to accomplish spiritual growth. So, for thousands of years people have accepted this false reality. They die without having accomplished evolution, and without ever finding out how to do so. You cannot evolve through the Bible any more than you can build a bridge by using the information contained in that book. How many more lifetimes do people want to spend defending their position that ducks equal wood?

When Columbus set sail, he did so in defiance of the accepted reality of his time. His Bible of the day told him that the world was flat. Most people had based their lives on this incorrect conclusion and were afraid that Columbus would fall off the face of the earth if he sailed too far away. Columbus challenged that reality, which is why he has become such a hero. If Columbus had not challenged reality, present-day Americans might still be sitting in Europe, living in fear of falling off the earth.

In order for anyone to grow, aspects of established reality must be challenged and truth must be established. This book is an attempt on the part of the Brotherhood to challenge current reality. If you do not want your reality challenged, then you should stop reading right here. It would be much more honest and decent to put this book down and admit that you want to preserve your reality, than to read the rest of the book and then have to use your resources to denounce it. The Brotherhood would prefer that you preserve your resources rather than consuming them to denounce this information or any information that is offered to help people grow by challenging their established systems.

GOD

When people talk about God or attempt to contact God through prayer, they are attempting to contact their human fantasies about God. Because these fantasies are not real there is no one listening to their prayers, regardless of their claims that their prayers have been answered. Because people are so preoccupied with their personal fantasies of God, they have no understanding of the real "God," or more accurately the Logos, of this planet. The Logos of this planet is the one who is responsible for the spiritual evolution of this planet. He is completely dedicated to helping humanity live more natural, correct, peaceful lives. Unfortunately, very few people are aware of his influence and presence because they are too filled up with religious fantasies.

People are much more interested in the glamour that can be found in religious rituals and self-proclaimed New Age gurus than they are in the Logos of this planet or the Plan for spiritual growth. Most people, in the course of their many lifetimes, have participated in many different religions. They have been Catholics, Protestants, Jews, Muslims, Hindus, Buddhists, and Communists (which the Brotherhood calls the world's largest religion). They have observed the priests and bishops in their long regal robes and tall head crowns, carrying their royal staffs. People have seen the pomp and ceremonial ado of the "high holy days," and the bowing and adoration given to the Muslim mullahs. To the human ego, these symbols of glamour have become signs of a spiritual presence.

The New Age enlightenment seekers want a modern version of these old religious ideas. They want their gurus, swamis, and bhagwans to wear white Indian robes, long hair, beards, and sandals. They think that their New Age symbols of glamour are actually spiritual because they are more "simple" or because their gurus speak in more modern cliches about "light and love." The New Age enlightenment seekers are exactly the same as the religious drug addicts. What they want are meditation exercises and New

Age cliches. They want a new kind of religious glamour, but they do not want spiritual growth.

If people wanted to know how to find God, they could first look at what their society's gentry will or will not support. Once people discover what the rich and powerful will support as spiritual, they can then eliminate that which is being supported as having anything to do with God or spiritual growth. For example, when Jesus lived on this planet, many prophets and gurus of that time were supported. Jesus, however, lived in poverty. He was not glamourous. He did not dress in flashy robes nor did he say popular things. He healed a very limited number of people with the spiritual powers available to him at that time. He understood his personal mission and had no intention of becoming a Bible hero. Unfortunately, people have turned Jesus into a legend and have, therefore, lost any understanding of what he was attempting to do spiritually.

Today, there are people on this planet who are more evolved than Jesus and who have more available spiritual healing power. They, like Jesus, are extremely ordinary people whose work remains quiet and unsupported by humanity because these people are not glamourous nor are they righteous. The more spiritualized a person is, the less righteous and glamourous that person is. The wealthy people of today's society will support the televangelists, with their five hundred dollar suits, private universities, and expensive cars, because they are glamourous and righteous. People will send thousands of dollars to righteous people who are not healing anyone. They will spend hundreds of dollars to hear Ramtha at a weekend seminar. They will listen to Ramtha, a rambling third degree initiate, as though he were God, because Ramtha offers meaningless cliches to help people stay asleep and passive.

The gentry of any society at any time will only support those "spiritual endeavors" that will maintain the status quo and insure their positions of power and wealth. If Jesus were in incarnation today, he would be living much more like Mitch Snyder than like any of humanity's New Age gurus. Mitch Snyder struggles each day to provide food and shelter for needy people all over the United States. He is not supported by the gentry except when it is convenient and politically beneficial to them. Mitch Snyder has to beg and plead for help for his work every day, while people think nothing of spending a few hundred dollars for a weekend with a

Ramtha. So while New Age gurus collect cars and horses, Mitch Snyder collects homeless people. The money and the resources will not come forth to buy food and shelter for the hungry and homeless. People would much rather keep their gurus supplied with houses, horses, and cars than to support people who are actually traveling on a spiritual path.

People cannot find God because they are looking for righteousness and glamour. When people are growing spiritually and offering real aid, they do not become more righteous and more glamourous. They become less and less of everything through a natural detachment from the human world that will be discussed later in this book.

EVOLUTION

Evolution is a process of spiritual growth that is directed and engineered by the individual soul. The Logos of this planet is responsible for the Plan to restore this planet to a Path of evolution. Evolution is a process of continuous, ongoing change that occurs within a person's soul. Change, in this sense, is not random, like a change in traffic flow or the weather. Rather, it is specific change engineered by the soul to produce specific spiritual growth and learning.

People often feel disconnected from God. And they are. They are disconnected from their own souls and are therefore separated from the process of evolution. Because they are only connected to their personal fantasies about God, people actually feel that there is no God. Even the most ardent Catholics and devout Jews do not feel connected to God. They only pretend to be connected in their minds. They feel nothing of God in their hearts.

When people are evolving and growing spiritually, they experience a linkage with their own souls and with the spiritual realities of this planet, including the Logos. They do not need prayers, rituals, or religious fantasies to support their mental illusions. When people are evolving, they know and experience the real thing, a genuine connection to a real God. Unfortunately, only a handful of souls on this planet are actually engaged in the process of evolution.

Neither religion nor science has anything to offer humanity about the process of evolution, because neither religion nor science is based on an accurate body of information. The scientific belief system maintains that evolution occurs in the physical world and that man was once some lower form of animal. Evolution, however, is not a physical world process. Despite modern scientific theory, people were never apes. Evolution is a nonphysical world process, or spiritual process, that involves the growth and learning of the human soul.

Science is dedicated to studying the physical world. The scientific method teaches people to ignore anything that cannot be observed through the five senses. The scientific method has allowed science to become a kind of religion run by so-called experts who work only in the observable physical world. Scientists know almost nothing about subatomic structures. Since the soul is composed of subatomic structures, science remains ignorant of the existence of the human soul.

Scientists refuse to acknowledge that they know so little. They are human and therefore prefer to think they are very intelligent. They like the power and control over people's lives that their roles as scientists have given them. They use their positions to support incorrect theories and ideas because those theories allow them to remain in dominant roles. They avoid exploring information that could potentially lead people to understand the existence of their own souls and the real, nonphysical process of evolution. Instead, science teaches people that they were once monkeys who must now continue using their "human" intelligence to succeed in the human world, without regard for the existence of their souls. Scientists believe that this form of human success and human advancement has something to do with the process of evolution. It does not. If anything, human intellectual and technological success only causes people to become more enamored with human success and less concerned about spiritual growth.

Religions teach belief in the nonphysical world. However, these beliefs have nothing to do with spiritual reality. Religious leaders believe that people live in physical bodies for only a single lifetime. Religions teach people about personal salvation rather than individual evolution. This means that as long as people "practice" the rituals of a given religion they will be guaranteed a heavenly afterlife. This approach requires nothing of people. It causes people to believe they have only one chance at life and therefore must strive to become a human success. When people believe they have only one "chance" at human life, they spend their lives attempting to fulfill all of their human goals and ideas, without any regard for the spiritual purpose of each lifetime. People actually get more "chances" at human lifetimes than anyone would want to have.

Evolution is a process of spiritual growth that occurs over many human lifetimes. People have many opportunities to live in physical bodies. In actuality, people have far more opportunities than most of them would want if they really understood what was happening on this planet. Religions teach people that their "eternal" time will be spent in some afterlife rather than teaching people that their time will be spent right here in the physical world until they have earned a level of evolution that no longer requires physical incarnations.

The physical world exists for the purpose of providing an environment where evolution can take place. This is the only real purpose for the physical universe. When people are able to use the physical universe for its intended purpose, they are then able to learn and to grow spiritually. The learning that must be accomplished has nothing to do with the human mind or the physical brain. In fact, the human mind is far too limited to accomplish soul evolution. This learning has much more to do with a person's ability to make connections and understand how the world actually works. Modern education has destroyed humanity's ability to grow spiritually by causing children to study unrelated, disconnected things in a way that destroys the natural human ability to connect up with the way the world works. Religions have also drawn people's focus away from real spiritual learning and growing. Instead, they have captured human egos with illusions of guilt and fear.

Today, ninety-eight percent of this planet is unevolved and uninitiated. People incarnate into lives of meaninglessness, hurt and suffering without any purpose or learning. Most souls will take thousands and thousands of years to learn what could be accomplished in a few lifetimes, or even a single lifetime. Evolution, for most people, is now completely accidental. People are using the physical world only to fulfill empty, human goals. Religions function to keep things this way. Religions never speak of evolution or spiritual growth. Religions never provide people with accurate information about how spiritual growth is accomplished. Religions are too busy luring people with fantasies of heavenly reward and frightening them with threats of eternal damnation to provide the help people need to resume the process of evolution. To the human ego, salvation and damnation mean exactly the same thing. Both produce passivity and inertia without any spiritual growth whatsoever.

Evolution involves a process of steps or stages in spiritual growth known as the seven planetary initiations. Each initiation is taken only after an individual soul has accomplished the necessary requirements for that particular step. These requirements are set by spiritual law. Spiritual law is nothing like the Ten Commandments, as religions would have people believe. (The Ten Commandments were given to Moses as a guideline for human beings living in a human world. Unfortunately, no one on this planet obeys the Ten Commandments.)

Each soul exists only to fulfill his or her own unique purpose. Each soul, then, advances through evolution in his or her own unique way. So, although the requirements for initiations are governed by spiritual law, the method or way of accomplishing these requirements is different for each individual soul. When the Brotherhood says there are many roads of evolution, they are referring to the fact that each soul has a unique way of accomplishing spiritual growth. There is only one Great Way, however. People should not be fooled by old religious ideas and New Age spiritual trash claiming that there are many methods, techniques or rituals that can help people grow. None of the religious rituals of today provide a way of accomplishing the seven planetary initiations. Nor do any of the New Age roads to "enlightenment" provide a way of accomplishing initiations beyond the second—no matter how much "light and love" they claim to offer.

Each level of initiation requires that more and more of the human personality, with all its ideas, emotions, and desires, be surrendered over to the soul. At each level of initiation, the individual soul becomes stronger and gains more influence over a person's life. As the spiritual part of the person becomes more of itself, the human part becomes less. At the first initiation people must bring the lower physical nature under control. At this stage people begin to gain respect for one another and for themselves. They begin to gain control over self-righteousness, greed, and acts of physical violence.

At the second initiation people begin to gain control over their emotional aggressions. Because they have mastered a very basic control over their emotions, they are able to have control over their lives in the physical world. Second degree initiates are often very competent. Unfortunately, they can use their competence and ability to control their human lives in ways that often produce much human success and comfort. Human comfort is spiritually deadly because it causes a person to lose the spiritual ambition necessary for continued growth through change.

The third initiation requires that people open their hearts. This is very difficult to do in a world full of pain and suffering. People learn to live in their minds. When they open their hearts, they see the suffering, pain and emptiness in humanity. Usually third degree initiates on a spiritual path are drawn to some form of service, because they cannot look at humanity's pain without trying to do something to alleviate it.

The third step is the most dangerous point in evolution. At this step, the human ego has about fifty percent of the control over the human vehicle while the soul has gained the other fifty percent. At this stage the human ego and the soul battle one another for control over the person's life. The human ego is constantly being bombarded by human allurements of glamour, success, prestige, power and money. Third degree initiates enjoy a certain amount of personal power by virtue of their level of spiritual accomplishment. They often end up using their personal power to accomplish human goals and desires rather than to continue a path of spiritual growth.

When Jesus went into the desert, he was at the third initiation. He was facing all the human allurements or temptations. He was undergoing the test of power that every third degree initiate must face. He had to distinguish the empty mirages of human satisfaction from genuine spiritual fulfillment. Having passed this test and fulfilled these requirements, he was prepared to take the fourth initiation. He did this at the time of his death.

At the fourth initiation the soul gains about seventy-five percent control over the human vehicle. Here people relinquish their human goals and desires. At this stage the soul enters the Brotherhood and must begin a path of service. Fourth degree initiates usually live somewhat secluded from other people because their vibration is so much higher than the rest of humanity that "normal" human life is no longer possible. At the fifth initiation a person breaks from the physical world completely. Most fourth and fifth degree initiates accomplish these levels of spiritual growth at physical death, although physical death is no longer essential for upward spiritual movement. At the fifth initiation the lower mental-emotional bodies drop away. The soul body is reclaimed and the spirit or Monad directs the person's life. The Monad might be thought of as a soul's actual source or one's own personal God.

Fifth degree initiates no longer carry any illusions about the physical world. They see it for what it is and therefore do not need to continue their growth in the physical world. At this level reincarnation is no longer necessary. Spiritual growth from this point on is a matter of achieving higher states of spiritual perfection.

Sixth and seventh degree initiates represent the Logos of this planet in some way. There are very few fifth, sixth or seventh degree initiates living on this planet. Those who do are very secluded and not in contact with the general world population. They do not include any priest, minister, rabbi or religious leader on this planet today, regardless of any such claim. There are no religious leaders representing God or the Logos. They are all representing themselves.

To accomplish spiritual growth under the shield or protection of the Brotherhood, a person must have access to the wisdom and perfection achieved by a seventh degree initiate. Since seventh degree initiates generally do not live in the physical world, it is necessary for uninitiated people to connect up with first and second degree initiates who are connected to others who are connected to a seventh degree initiate. This chain of command represents the governing body of this planet called Planetary Hierarchy.

RELIGIOUS LEADERSHIP vs. SPIRITUAL LEADERSHIP

All religious leaders today have emerged from the human world. There have been great men and women such as Jesus, Muhammad, and others who came to offer humanity spiritual leadership. However, neither Jesus nor Muhammad was attempting to offer humanity a religion. Each of these men came to teach a small group of people a specific lesson and to accomplish some of the requirements necessary for their own individual evolution. People then took these lessons and distorted them to fit their own fantasies. They turned Jesus and Muhammad into legends, and perverted their teachings to form present-day religions. Neither Jesus nor Muhammad intended to become a religious folk hero. They were spiritually ambitious souls attempting to teach no more than a few hundred people about the reality of spiritual evolution.

Religious leaders are never spiritual leaders. They are always human egos representing their own needs for power and control. They are not, in any way, representatives of the Logos of this planet. Religious leaders seek their positions in order to obtain the social protection offered to them in their roles as rabbis, ministers, nuns, and priests. When a person becomes a member of the clergy, society places a veil over that person that prevents other people from seeing what the person is actually like. People then project onto that veil all of the qualities they would want a nun or priest, for example, to possess. Once this occurs, no one ever questions or confronts the priest or nun's actual behaviors, relationships, mental stability, or general lifestyle. Everyone treats the priest as though he were his role as a "priest" rather than as himself.

This societal veil allows very sick and disturbed people to enter the "religious life." It allows many people who might otherwise require serious psychiatric care to function in protected societal roles without having any of their mental-emotional instability challenged. These roles allow clergymen and women to do anything and to say anything without facing any of the normal life confrontations that bring about behavior change.

If people could have seen their current religious leaders as children between the ages of eight and ten, they would better understand the functioning of this protective veil. Between these ages, most of today's religious leaders were alienated, disturbed children who were unable to relate to their classmates and friends in normal, healthy ways. They were not alienated because they were "special" children or because God had already chosen them for a religious calling. They were alienated because they were sick. They were alienated because they were suffering from lifetimes of unhealed mental-emotional damage. Somewhere along the line, they discovered that they could remain sick, obtain great power, and still function within society by becoming clergy.

If people wanted to better understand their religious leaders, they could make a list of those qualities that they believe a priest, minister or rabbi should possess. Then they would know something about how the societal veil is constructed. Next, people could make a list of all the qualities one would not want to find in a religious leader, such as greed, selfishness, personal isolation, power-hunger, or self-righteousness. The second list would more accurately describe over ninety percent of those men and women now claiming to offer spiritual leadership.

Real spiritual leaders provide selfless service. They exist primarily in the nonphysical world. When they do come to humanity, they come like Jesus and Muhammad to groups of people who can benefit from a particular message at a particular time. Real spiritual leaders do not have to lie about life or about why people are here. They do not require special seats in restaurants or reduced clergy air fares. They do not want to be called "Your Excellency" or "Your Eminence" because they already have real royalty and do not need religious glamour.

Religious leaders have no access to the Brotherhood or to Planetary Hierarchy. They are far too committed to protecting their own personal problems to be able to connect to a chain of evolving souls. For the most part, they are too alienated and sick themselves to be able to provide anyone with even human comfort and relief.

The people who carry the most hatred and the lowest ideas about humanity are the ones who generally rise to the top of their religious organizations and churches. Almost all of the current televangelists carry animosity toward humanity. They use their positions and their words to beat other people with their own ideas and antagonism in the same way that alcoholics beat people in their environment with their alcoholism.

Most of the evangelical, pentecostal, and other extremist religions are led by people who want to inflict hatred. These ministers are the ones who give people a long list of "don'ts" and convince them that they are sinners. They pound on people with words so that people will feel very negative about themselves. Then they give people the only "do" that their religions have to offer—"do send money." These ministers convince people that the only way they can be saved from themselves is by contributing money. These so-called religious leaders are not saving millions of souls. They are saving millions of dollars. Their medical missions, universities, and hunger projects are only gimmicks for making money. It is not as if none of these funds are used to help needy people because, indeed, some people are receiving food and medical supplies. However, the primary interests of these religious leaders have nothing to do with these projects. Without these "cover" projects, people would not send millions of dollars to buy expensive cars and homes for televangelists.

These ministers boast of saving millions of souls. There is no basis in reality for these claims. A saved soul, by modern religion's own definition, is someone who goes to church and finds peace of mind through the practice of a religion. An alcoholic who stops drinking, but uses the Bible to beat up on his family in the same way that he once used the bottle, is not a saved soul. A former prostitute who stops using her body to hook people, and instead uses religion to hook them, is not a saved soul. People who get relief from certain problems due to the passage of time are not saved souls. About two-thirds of the people who say that religion brought them relief from their problems would have gotten relief no matter what they did. In fact, if they had spent their Sunday mornings on the beach or in the grocery store, they would not only have experienced relief from their problems; they would also have avoided collecting the new set of negative thoughts and ideas about themselves that they picked up by listening to condemning sermons in church.

For all their boasting, these religious leaders have not saved souls. They have only collected and "saved" their followers' money. Even though many television ministers are being publicly questioned for their actions and lifestyles, it is very unlikely that such challenges will be sustained. People will drift back into their fantasies of saved souls while their ministers continue to save their own personal fortunes.

THE PATHOLOGY OF RELIGION

Each of the major world religions was founded out of the damages and human suffering of its original members. Each religion attracts leaders who can best perpetuate that damage. All religious rituals offer more of the same damage.

It is bad enough that religions are nothing more than made-up human fantasies. It is tragic enough to have people so preoccupied with these fantasies that they are unable to grow spiritually. Worse yet is the fact that many people cannot shake loose from these lies even at physical death. Their ideas and expectations for heaven or hell are so strong that they refuse to take the help offered at physical death by the Brotherhood, which could lead them to places of rest and learning. Some spend thousands of years on the lower astral planes looking for "pearly gates" that do not exist, or for some other made-up afterlife fantasy. These illusions in and of themselves have caused human suffering beyond belief.

However, religions offer not only fantasies. They also offer damage and sickness. Whenever a person seriously follows a religion, that person carries the pathology of that religion in his or her consciousness. We will discuss the individual pathologies in the chapters ahead. By inflicting further damage on people through fear and guilt, religions have destroyed many human ego structures. Many people have been damaged by religion to the extent that these structures are rendered useless to the soul. Religions have left millions of people beyond repair. And, as We have said, some will not accept help even at death.

If you belong to a religion, you can think of yourself as someone who has joined a club, like a country club, fraternity, or garden club. When people join a club, they usually do so because they want to be associated with the "right" people. The "right" club members usually see themselves as separate from and better than other people who do not belong to their particular club.

When people join religions, they believe they are members of a special club of "chosen" people. They go to meetings and believe that their club offers them, and only them, personal salvation and eternal reward. The Catholics, for example, believe that they have found the one true religion club. The Jews believe that being born into the Jewish club makes them the chosen people. The Muslims believe that the Muslim club is the way to salvation. Even the Communists, who are not generally seen as a religious group, have a religious club. They have their own "Bible" written by Karl Marx, and their own Jesus which they call "comradeship." Comradeship is worshiped in exactly the way that Christians worship Jesus.

Communists believe that through the Communism club they will be saved in the same way that the Christian club members believe they are saved through Jesus.

There are Methodist clubs, Baptist clubs, Lutheran clubs and Buddhist clubs. They are as useless to evolution as a country club or sorority. When people join religion clubs, they are not motivated by a common desire for spiritual growth. They join out of a common pathology and desire for religious fantasy. They get no more spiritual help from a religion club than they would get from joining a bowling league. In fact, the information and learning about life offered at a bowling alley is far more likely to be accurate than anything they will ever hear in church.

Since this book is part of an evolutionary project working primarily with people in Western societies, this material will focus on the major religion clubs of the Western world, with the exception of Islam. It should be understood that all religions are products of the human world just like country clubs, garden clubs, the Lions clubs, Kiwanis, and Elks Lodges. Religions, including New Age "paths" to enlightenment, which We might best call the Enlightenment clubs or the "Light and Love" clubs, are leading people further into passivity and inertia no matter what they claim to be doing or where they operate in the world.

2

JUDAISM
The Jewish Club

THE HISTORY OF the Jewish people is a long one of separateness and separation. Judaism began with a small group of nomadic people who were seeking relief from the hurts of separation and nomadic life. These homeless souls were energetically drawn together because each one individually had suffered many prior lifetimes of separation from others. Although each one suffered his or her own unique pain, the damages to each consciousness were very similar in their energetic nature. These damages acted like magnetic fields drawing these souls together in corresponding pain.

If this planet had not been in the midst of an endarkened era, these people might have provided one another with some comfort and support. They might have been able to settle and form families and some sort of real community life together. Because the time of Darkness left humanity with little ability to heal their damages, people simply carried those damages from one lifetime to another, continuing to attract damaging situations over and over again without any relief.

As a group these early Jews were severely damaged people. They would have been considered seriously disturbed by current mental health standards. They had lost all connection to the land and for the correct establishment of home and family. They had lost their ability and natural desire to relate and to establish correct relationships. There was nothing available to help these people lift themselves out of their personal pain. They had no means or resources to alter the course of their lives.

Out of damage and hurt they formed the Jewish faith or club. They became the founding fathers of a religion club that would not only perpetuate their pain and damage, but would actually inflict the same agony on those who followed the way of Judaism— the religion club of separation.

This group of nomadic souls formed early rituals and beliefs in an attempt to comfort themselves. They attracted many others who suffered from similar feelings of separateness and disconnectedness. They turned to their minds in an attempt to solve the problems of their hearts. They wrote and read books rather than relating to one another. They became a "persecuted" and homeless group instead of being persecuted and homeless individuals. They remained disconnected from the land and from establishing the roots they all needed. They formed distorted ideas about spiritual support, the roles of men and women, the proper raising of children, and the meaning of a successful life.

Judaism has nothing to do with God. It is as purposeless and aimless as its founding fathers. It is built on pathology and it produces pathology in anyone who takes it seriously. Judaism damages people and prevents them from growing spiritually.

Some would claim that these statements are anti-Semitic. They would be partially correct. The Brotherhood is "anti-Semitic" in the sense that they are against any religion club inflicting damages on humanity in the name of God. The Jewish people who claim anti-Semitism are attempting to protect their damages. Some know how hurt they are, but do not want to see that they have wasted their lives on something so dark. They do not want to admit that they have been fooled by their parents, relatives and rabbis. Others are so invested in their damages that they live in tiny dark worlds of Jewish tradition and ritual. They use all their available resources to maintain these dark little worlds.

The more a person follows the religious laws and traditions of

Judaism, the more seriously he or she is disturbed. The extremely devoted orthodox groups are the most disturbed of all. They are most like Judaism's founding fathers. They suffer the greatest damage and have the least ability to relate to others and to the world. Some of these people would be institutionalized if they did not have the boundaries of Judaism to contain their pathology. They are the people most likely to be incited by this book and the work of the Brotherhood, because they have their pathologies so well protected.

The damages and hurts of Judaism's early founders are the only real Jewish heritage. These damages are manifested every day in the rituals of the Jewish religion and, even more tragically, in the lives of millions of Jewish people. The founding nomads' disconnectedness from the earth, the pain of separation from other people, and the mental compensation for these hurts form the Jewish religion club of today.

THE RITUALS OF SEPARATION

Each day millions of Jews throughout the world continue to act out their hurt and pain in rituals of separation. These rituals are the physical manifestations of the hurt suffered by Judaism's founding fathers. Every day millions of Jews act out this pathology in an attempt to make it something sacred and holy. There is nothing holy about damage, and nothing sacred in any of these rituals. There is serious sickness and disturbance in many who practice them.

In the temple, men and women are sometimes still seated separately. Women are seated off to the side or up in a balcony that overlooks the service, while men are given the favored seats. Men participate in the service; women observe. Men can touch the "sacred" Torah. Women cannot.

Women are kept separate because they are considered inferior to men, particularly intellectually. This separate seating arrangement and the underlying belief system have caused and continue to cause serious relationship problems for Jewish men and women everywhere. It causes Jewish couples to suffer personal loneliness and isolation from one another to such a serious extent that most

Jewish men and women are numb and unconscious about their own isolation. They actually accept their conditions as normal and act as if their broken-down relationships are healthy.

In times past, menstruating women were kept apart from their husbands. Menstruating women were seen as unclean and unacceptable. These attitudes are still embedded in Jewish women today, and negatively affect the menstrual cycles, childbearing experiences and sex lives of Jewish women everywhere.

Jewish children are taught to see themselves as separate and different from other children. This idea that they are separate and different from other children often translates into the idea that they are better than other children. This throws the human personalities of many Jewish children into a polarity in which they are either looking down on others or feeling inferior to others. Neither polarity produces a healthy, functioning child.

Jewish children and teenagers are encouraged to join temple groups that provide them with separate, private social lives. They are taught to date other Jews and not to seek non-Jewish marriage partners. Interfaith marriage is frowned upon by many Jewish families and even condemned by others. If a Jewish man or woman attempts to break from the Jewish legacy of damage by marrying a non-Jew, he or she may suffer another kind of hurt from the condemnations of the family. In attempting to break from the darkness and damage caused by isolation, those who marry non-Jews are just hurt by another kind of alienation from their parents and others who may have been close to them.

Many Jewish people maintain a separate calendar and observe separate holidays which continue to keep them apart from the larger society. Some Jewish people separate their foods into Kosher and non-Kosher products. They believe it is unholy to mix meat and dairy. They believe they can actually grow spiritually if they keep their chicken and cheese on separate plates. Some believe that it is wrong to eat seafood unless it has gills and fins, or to eat meat unless it is from animals that chew their cud and have cloven hoofs. They keep separate dishes and pans and follow lists of absurd practices in the preparation of their foods. Most of these practices would be diagnosed as psychotic disturbances under any other conditions.

These procedures are as disturbed as Judaism's founding fathers.

They are as aimless and purposeless as the original nomads. They are nothing more than acted out damages that have been proclaimed sacred by seriously disturbed people. The Jewish people have not found comfort in these rituals. They have not found relief for their personal problems and pain. Nor have they found emotional support. These practices have nothing to do with emotional growth or physical health. They are not holy practices, and they definitely do not nurture the soul of anyone. So, what are Jewish people doing in the name of God?

THE RABBIS

In the Jewish club, men become rabbis because they have the ability to lead people into rituals and ideas that perpetuate their alienation. Like all religious leaders, rabbis want personal power to give them control over the lives of other people. As with other religious leaders, rabbis use the power to cover up and protect their own unresolved personal problems, and to carry on the pathology inherent in the religion itself.

As children, most would-be rabbis live very isolated, lonely lives. They are usually raised by strict Jewish parents who practice the Judaic rituals of alienation, often to the extreme. Rabbis are usually products of disturbed parents with disturbed marriage relationships. These parents tend to use the Jewish religion club to cover up their personal damages and to protect the problems in their marriage relationships. In this way they offer their sons perfect role models of how someone can use the Jewish religion to protect themselves from facing their problems.

Rabbis usually receive all the traditional training in separateness and are taught to see themselves as apart from and better than other people. They often attend Hebrew school and confine their generally limited social life to temple-sponsored activities. For the most part, they tend to be very lonely and unable to relate to another human being in healthy, meaningful ways. To compensate for their loneliness and detachment, they retreat into their minds. They are inclined to live in books and materials they can read, rather than in the real world with real people. Usually they are good students with good memories who receive recognition for their intelligence. In a way they are very much like the founding fathers of Judaism. Although they are not wandering in the desert in search of a homeland, they are wandering aimlessly in their minds and thoughts. They have become mental nomads who have no home in reality.

When men become rabbis, no one expects them to be able to relate to people in healthy ways. They are not expected to be able to form correct human relationships that could potentially heal their personal damages and loneliness. Rabbis are not expected to know much about home maintenance and repair, electrical wiring, plumbing or any physical world skills that could help them become grounded back into the real world. They are expected only to remain mental nomads who have nothing but empty words to offer millions of damaged souls. They are the Jewish religion club leaders because they have the ability to read and memorize meaningless books that have nothing to do with relieving human problems and suffering, and even less to do with any form of spiritual growth.

In their roles as rabbis, Jewish religious leaders can keep all their personal damages protected. They never have to look at themselves. They are well protected from the necessity of forming any kind of healthy human relationship. They can keep all their personal problems and proceed to inflict similar damage upon the members of their congregations, because they remain protected by the societal veil afforded to all clergymen and women.

Through their jobs the rabbis can encourage people to practice disturbed rituals in the name of religion. They can use their power and mental ability to convince people that these practices are sacred and will produce spiritual growth. They can remind the Jewish people to think of themselves as separate from and better than other people. They can encourage people to study books and teachings that will keep them as aimless and purposeless as Judaism's founding fathers.

Rabbis can remind Jewish people of their history and teach them to glorify their homelessness and persecution so the results of Judaism's damage can be praised and honored. They can teach Jewish people to remember always the Holocaust, which only perpetuates human suffering. The rabbis and many Jews would claim that if they keep the Holocaust alive they can prevent such a tragedy from ever recurring. If this is so, where were the Jews during the 1970s when Pol Pot was slaughtering thousands of Cambodians in the killing fields? Where are the Jews now, when blacks suffer daily persecutions in South Africa? The rabbis are not rallying Jewish people throughout the world to come to the aid of humanity. They are rallying Jewish people to remain isolated, alienated and, in some cases, disturbed. The rabbis are not attempting to find a technology that would provide psychological relief to the victims of the Holocaust and their families. They are attempting to use the pain and agony of this nightmare to keep Jewish people separate from others in humanity while they learn to glorify their personal pain.

The Jewish people have no idea what they are causing by using the memory of the Holocaust to perpetuate their alienation. By keeping this event alive, the Jewish people energetically create thoughtforms about the Holocaust that keep alive the energy which caused the Holocaust in the first place. They dramatically increase the likelihood of such an event occurring in the future. These thoughtforms are so strong that many souls, once victims of the Holocaust and now caught on the lower astral planes, believe that the Holocaust is still taking place.

JEWISH MEN

Jewish men are generally disconnected from the world in which they live and from the people around them. Because spiritual evolution requires people to use the physical world to make connections and to learn through relating to other people, most Jewish men are completely unable to grow spiritually. They are caught in the same darkness and disconnectedness as their forefathers, and cannot see what their Jewish heritage is costing them.

From the time they are very young, Jewish boys are encouraged to use their minds rather than their hearts. They are urged to develop their minds, to study hard, and to seek higher education. They are not taught or expected to relate in healthy ways to other children, or to have any real understanding of the world around them.

For the most part, Jewish boys and men do very well in current educational systems. They do well, however, because formal education fosters unrelatedness. Formal education encourages children to use their minds to memorize meaningless data and misinformation. Education does not teach children how to properly relate to the world in which they live. For example, most high school students have no idea how the books, pencils and desks are made that they use every day. They do not know how a book is typeset or bound, or how trees are turned into paper. They are unaware of the source of the lead in their pencils, or from what kind of wood their desks are made. They do not know how their classrooms are electrically wired or the origin of the electrical power. They know nothing about the plumbing system in the school. They have never used their geometry courses to discover that their surroundings are constructed of angles and shapes. Most students graduate from high school without the ability to change a fuse, repair a broken toilet or build anything of real value with their hands. Jewish men do very well in this educational system because it does not ask them to become correctly connected to anything.

In addition to causing this dissociation from the real world, education does not teach children anything about why they are alive or what they are doing on this planet. It offers no skills to help children become better husbands, wives or parents. Education provides no understanding about the sources of human problems, or any encouragement to children who will one day be faced with solving these problems. Formal education offers a perfect system to Jewish men who want to remain cut off from real life. The further along in the system a person goes, the more disconnected he or she becomes.

Jewish men are often successful in life. Many become doctors and lawyers who are professionally successful people. In the human sense these are successful professions, particularly if success is measured in dollars and cents. However, Jewish men excel in these professions because they are so detached from other people and from the problems of humanity. Jewish men make excellent physicians because they are completely disconnected from their patients' pain. They have the memorization ability necessary to complete medical school, and the alienation from people required to dispense modern medicine. They do not enter the field of medicine to serve humanity. They become physicians primarily to make money. Generally, they have no investment in actually solving the physical problems that people face. They are interested only in treating those problems. Their investments are in the banks and stock market, and most of them would much rather hear from their stockbrokers than their ailing patients.

Jewish men usually make excellent lawyers as well. They enjoy the mental games that the law encourages them to play, and they have no connection to the fact that those games are played at people's emotional and psychological expense. They are much more interested in their fees for service than in justice or the well-being of their clients.

Jewish men avoid becoming electricians, plumbers, carpenters or welders because these professions are seen as inferior. These professions would actually lead them back into connecting with the physical world rather than the mental world. These trades offer exactly what most Jewish men need to know and understand, but also offer exactly what Jewish men want to avoid. Jewish men are content to hire whatever tradespeople might be necessary to repair and maintain their homes, while keeping themselves energetically detached from their environments in the same way as Judaism's founders.

In relationships, Jewish men normally lack the skills and the interest to relate to others in healthy ways. By the time most Jewish men reach adulthood, they have lost their natural instinct to relate and have established an isolated world of books, words and ideas. Although they may walk through the motions of relating, Jewish men suffer much personal isolation and loneliness. Because of their Jewish training they are too isolated in their minds to see the failure of their relationships, or to know the pain of separation from others. Sadly, they carry on the Jewish tradition of alienation and raise their own sons to become disconnected physicians and lawyers who live in a world that has nothing to do with reality on this planet.

JEWISH WOMEN

Jewish women, in the eyes of Judaism, are inferior to men. Traditionally, women deserved to sit off to the side or up in the balcony during temple services. They were not considered worthy of participation. They deserved to be observers only. Traditionally, Jewish women were not allowed to read the same books as men because they were considered intellectually inferior and unworthy. They were not allowed to touch the "sacred Torah," or even to consider a role of leadership in the Jewish religion club.

In some Jewish religion clubs today, women still sit off to the side or in the balcony during services. They are still allowed only to observe. Regardless of where they are sitting, Judaism still considers women inferior and fails to recognize them as having the same value as men.

Ironically, Jewish women have developed compensations for these damaging attitudes. For centuries, women looked down upon their men from above during temple services. They developed the "superior" idea or compensation that they were not only "above" Jewish men in the temple, but that they were above all of humanity. They generally view themselves as smarter than Jewish men because they understand that Jewish men live in tiny mental worlds that have nothing to do with reality. The women believe they should be catered to and waited on wherever they go. They expect to be treated better than other people.

Jewish women usually expect to be financially supported by their husbands and accept financial support as though it constituted a real relationship. They are likely to judge their relationships by what their husbands can provide for them rather than looking for what would produce a healthy, supportive marriage.

Jewish women do not expect healthy sexual relationships and often consider sex beneath them. Many Jewish women learn to use sex against their husbands as a way of punishing these men for their unhealthy attitudes toward Jewish women. Jewish men perpetuate these unhealthy attitudes. They are so incapable of relating from any part of themselves except their minds that they have turned sex into a mental act, void of all emotion and tenderness. In addition, Jewish women tend to view men as "little boys" because Jewish men insist on remaining detached and therefore incompetent regarding the realities of the physical, human world.

The damages inflicted by the religious practices of Judaism tend to cause many problems in the functioning of the male and female polarities. Jewish men are inclined to become unnaturally passive, while Jewish women compensate and become more dominant and aggressive. The resulting behaviors are unnatural to both men and women. These imbalances in the polarities are observed by Jewish children throughout childhood and are carried on for generations without the necessary repair.

Jewish women tend to be hurt and angry, which leads to bitterness and resentment when left unhealed. They often look for emotional support from their children when their children are young and in need of support themselves. Jewish women generally have very little genuine nurturing ability, despite the traditional myths of chicken soup and Jewish mothers. They are too hurt from being treated as inferiors; and the lack of adult support in their own lives makes them unable to provide any form of real nurturance to their children. Jewish women are likely to feel the impact of their personal loneliness in a very poignant way when their children become adults and leave home. These women are then faced with the travesty they have called marriage and the illusion of family. All that remains are their compensations for centuries of mistreatment by the Jewish religion club.

THE JEWISH FAMILY

The human system always views life in terms of polarities. The human ego tends to categorize people, places and events. For instance, each person creates categories of good people and bad people. There are "superior" professions and "inferior" professions. There are female roles and male roles. There is "us and them."

Because of the Judaic notion of separateness, Jewish families tend to energetically function on an "us and them" basis. That is to say, Jewish families think they must hold themselves together energetically no matter how bad things become because they view people outside the family as potential enemies. For centuries Judaism has taught Jewish people to think in paranoid ways, to view all others as potential enemies. The Holocaust and the events surrounding the Hitler regime only fed into this sickness, causing Jews to feel justified in their paranoid systems. The tortures of Nazi Germany caused Jewish families to become even more polarized in their "us and them" position—which is really "us *against* them."

Jewish parents teach their children that "family" must be placed above all else. What they are really saying is that the paranoid idea of us against them must be placed above all else. They are not at all invested in the individual well-being of family members, nor do they have any idea about what makes up a healthy parent-child relationship. They have only their idea of "family" which is, again, the idea of energetically bonding against outsiders.

In today's more sophisticated society, Jewish parents have many more sophisticated mental ideas of "family" which cover up the paranoia inherent in Judaism. These ideas even sound correct when they are verbalized. Some parents go through the motions of acting out these ideas of "family." Yet, very few Jewish families actually live in healthy, supportive systems.

Because Jewish parents—fathers especially—have so little ability to relate, their acts of affection and physical contact are only mental acts. These actions are rarely motivated by any real emotion or tenderness. Jewish children feel the emptiness being offered by their parents, but because they are unable to find anything real or wholesome they settle for mental ideas and mental acts. Young Jewish children feel the split between what their parents claim to be offering and what is actually being given. When healthy Jewish children complain about what is missing in their families, Jewish parents—especially the mothers—act as if they are being persecuted by their children. Any effort on the part of a Jewish child to expose the emptiness and paranoia in the system is met with disapproval and feigned martyrdom, leaving the child guilty and despairing.

If Jewish children persist in their efforts to expose the family, they are often taken to a psychotherapist. Because Jewish people believe they must "stick with their own kind," Jewish parents usually take their children to a Jewish psychiatrist or psychologist. Psychotherapists, as a group, are seriously disturbed people, as We have discussed in *The Psychology of Spiritual Growth*. Jewish psychotherapists are generally the most seriously disturbed of all psychotherapists. They have no ability to relate—as demonstrated in their personal lives—and they use their professions to protect serious personal damage and pathology. Jewish parents are so intent on keeping the Jewish tradition of emptiness and paranoia alive that they are willing to place potentially healthy children in the hands of seriously disturbed psychotherapists. They are willing to pay exorbitant fees to place their children in the hands of what the Brotherhood would call child abusers.

After several years in weekly psychotherapy sessions, most Jewish children are back on the road to insanity. The ones who never made it to the psychotherapist's office gave in without a fight. The ones who attended psychotherapy usually fought and lost. The net effect is that most Jewish children are programmed into pathology no matter how resistant they may be.

A few Jewish children grow up and try to break away from what they know is insanity. They socialize with non-Jewish adults. They date non-Jewish people. They even marry non-Jewish spouses. However, Jewish parents respond to these attempts with more disapproval. They continue to act as if they were being persecuted. They condemn their children's marriages. They may even break off all contact with their children, causing them much guilt and hurt. So, even though these young adults have attempted to free themselves from this insane system, they are still caught. They are caught in the polarity of rebellion which is only the opposite of doing what parents want and expect. They are not free. They are guilty. No matter what they say, they are guilty. They will either spend their lives guilty or swing back into doing what their parents want. Very few, if any, ever escape the damage. The pathological system is centuries old. It has not changed. It still works to keep Jewish people sick and damaged. It is a perfect example of the human way.

Because Judaism has taught Jewish people to view themselves as alienated from others, most Jewish people do not see themselves as being connected to the rest of the world. They do not see that they are a part of humanity. They energetically separate themselves from the pain and the problems of other people unless those problems relate directly to the Jewish community. This separation causes Jewish people to remain energetically isolated and disconnected from other people in the world who are actually suffering some of the same nightmares of political persecution against which Jews claim to stand. This idea of separation has prevented the Jewish people from relating to the Holocaust in Cambodia or to any of the political persecutions in South and Central America.

Jewish families are interested in educational groups and organizations that will keep the memory of the Holocaust alive. This is just another way of keeping Jews separate and special. In order to preserve the pathology of Judaism, Jewish people spend their financial resources perpetuating their own pain. They use their resources to memorialize and glorify a tragedy, rather than using their energies in any real attempt to prevent another one.

Many Jewish families support the Zionist movement rather than aiding the homeless or the hungry. Again, they will support a cause that keeps them alienated instead of connecting to other people, even in the same community or town. They would prefer to see themselves as fighting for a homeland than to make a real home with healthy connections to the land and earth and the real people around them.

Jewish people support Jewish causes. Unfortunately, they do not support Jewish causes that are in their best interest. If Jewish people really wanted to support a Jewish cause, they would establish special schools to teach Jewish people—men particularly—the necessary skills to help them begin relating to the physical world in a healthy way. These schools would offer basic courses in woodworking, electrical wiring and plumbing. They would teach Jewish men how to repair and maintain their homes. This would help Jewish families feel connected to their homes and put an end to the centuries of energetic disconnection and homelessness. These courses would help Jewish men reconnect with the use of their hands and the realities of the physical world around them, including the people with whom they live every day.

Unfortunately, this suggestion is not likely to be followed. The pathology of Judaism is very old. People have been protecting Judaism and using its rituals to protect their own disturbances for centuries. The Jewish people are not likely to change their ways easily, nor are they likely to comprehend the spiritual price they pay for belonging to the religion club of Judaism. At this time they are too preoccupied with their dedication to making pathology into something sacred to be able to accomplish any genuine spiritual growth. They are too involved with the rituals and ideas that protect their "pet" idea that they, the Jews, are the Chosen people. As long as they are the Chosen people, they have already been saved. They do not have to do anything about the fact that their marriages are a mess; that they are making their children sick;

and that they are becoming more and more disconnected from reality. Since they are the Chosen people, they can keep their stock portfolios. They can take money from people, like the patients who need their help, without regard for what these people can or cannot afford. Since they are the Chosen people they can continue to do whatever they want with their lives without regard for anyone else, because they have already been saved.

3

CATHOLICISM
The Catholic Club

THE CATHOLIC CLUB has its roots in Judaism and in the idea of being a chosen people. Catholics have decided, however, that they, and they alone, are members of the one true religion club. Catholicism is the religion of grandiosity. Its members believe they are so important that Jesus died so they, the Catholics, would be saved. It is never clear exactly from what the Catholics have been saved. It is clear that the Catholics believe they have been saved from doing any of the hard work associated with evolution, and that they are free to do whatever they wish with their lives. Catholics believe they are exempt from all personal responsibility for spiritual growth because Jesus has already saved them. This pathological grandiosity prevents Catholic club members from being able to grasp any aspect of spiritual reality.

When Catholics do commit a wrong, or "sin" as they call it, they simply go to confession. At confession they receive absolution, which in their minds relieves them of any responsibility for the sins they have committed and provides them with a clean slate, free of all karmic debt. Since absolution can readily be obtained, most Catholics feel completely comfortable about repeating the same hurtful behaviors. They believe they can always go to confession and obtain forgiveness. They simply say their penance and are free to go, except where sex is concerned. The Catholic religion club uses sex to control people, as We will discuss later in this chapter.

Catholics have completely lost any understanding of cause and effect. Their grandiose fantasies prevent them from grasping the reality of karmic law. Everything in the human world must be balanced. If someone spends a lifetime in extreme wealth, it is very likely that in another life that same soul will experience the other side of wealth—abject poverty. If wealthy people understood the karmic law of energetic balance, they would not turn their backs on the poor.

If a person spends a lifetime in an executive position with much power over others' lives and mismanages that power, very likely that same soul will experience the other side of his or her own cruelty and mismanagement at another time. If a husband or wife abuses his or her spouse in one lifetime, the law of karma or balance will cause that soul to experience abuse in a future lifetime.

The law of balance or karma is not a system of reward and punishment. It is a system of spiritual growth and evolution. There is no one enforcing this law because, by nature, the law enforces itself. What a person sows, a person reaps. Catholic religious fantasies prevent any understanding of this law. Confession and absolution do not answer the law of karma or balance. Catholic religious fantasies actually cause people to lose their basic connection between cause and effect.

Once a person has lost his or her understanding of this simple, natural law, evolution becomes impossible. All growth ceases until the person can once again re-establish a system of cause and effect. Most Catholics are so damaged by their religious fantasies that cause and effect cannot be re-established for many, many lifetimes.

Another way of looking at this problem is to watch the way that Corazon Aquino of the Philippines has been paraded around by Catholics as an example of someone who has achieved her political position through her Catholic faith. Corazon Aquino did not become strong through her religion. If Catholicism produced the strength and sincerity found in Cory Aquino then many more

Catholics would demonstrate the same admirable qualities. In fact, there are now many more Catholics poisoning and pillaging the environment than leading countries out of suppression and poverty. Many more Catholics are suffering from alcoholism, mental illness, and chronic physical diseases than are dedicated to helping a country repair its wounds and damages. If the Catholic club gave people strength and courage, Catholics all over the world would rally to help Cory Aquino repair her country. She would not have to waste her valuable time and resources visiting the United States and playing political begging games for money. If the Catholics want to parade Cory Aquino around, let them also parade Marcos and his wife, and her three thousand pairs of shoes. Let them parade the millions of Catholics who abuse their children emotionally and physically, who cheat on their spouses, lie to their friends, gossip about their neighbors, and fail to pay their honest share of income taxes. However, they will not do that because they are too busy constructing another grandiose illusion—the illusion that Catholicism breeds women like Mrs. Aquino.

In reality (something in which Catholics are not interested) Cory Aquino is a fourth degree initiate. Her husband, Benigno, was a first degree initiate who completely understood his personal destiny. People see sincerity and honesty in Mrs. Aquino, but not because she is a practicing Catholic. They see a woman with an open heart who is speaking from her heart. They see someone who is speaking from her heart because of her level of spiritual accomplishment as a third degree initiate, not because of her religious ideas. Cory Aquino is much more dedicated to serving her people than she is to Catholicism. When she says that her strength comes from her religion, she really means from her own soul and from her own spiritual evolution.

Catholicism never produces strength. Rather, it weakens and destroys people through fear and guilt. Catholicism never produces sincerity or integrity, because it is a system that is built on lies and made-up fantasies. Catholicism has nothing to do with democracy, human rights, or peace. Catholicism has never had anything to do with these things. In fact, Catholicism has a long history of religious wars, violence, and human destruction.

To say that Catholicism is responsible for producing a woman like Cory Aquino is like saying that the American Dairy Association is responsible for producing a man like Charles Manson because Manson drank milk until he was a teenager. It is obvious, perhaps, that the American Dairy Association did not cause Manson to become a mass murderer. However, in the Catholic consciousness cause and effect are destroyed so completely that Catholics and even ex-Catholics who read this information will still credit Catholicism with producing Mrs. Aquino.

It should be noted here that the only country using Catholicism in any positive way at this time is Poland. The Polish people are using the "Church" as a focal point for Solidarity. Therefore, the energy involved is now being directed away from religious lies and fantasies toward the reality of much needed solidarity. In all other countries the Catholic religion is used to consume energy and resources and prevents the people from acting for peace, democracy and human rights.

JESUS

Every religion begins with a key or lead idea. Once you buy that idea, you buy the whole system. The key idea is always a magical idea that has no basis in reality. Once people buy the magical idea which is based in illusion, the religious leaders can tell people anything they want to tell them.

The key idea for Catholicism is the Immaculate Conception. Jesus was not conceived through a cosmic phenomenon. Jesus was conceived through normal sexual intercourse, and born to good but uninitiated parents. The Immaculate Conception is considered a dogma of the Catholic club, which means that people must accept this ridiculous fantasy under pain of mortal sin. Once they do accept this magical idea, Catholicism is free to feed people any other illusions.

Jesus did live on earth for some twenty-five years (not thirty-three). He did come to serve humanity in a very small way. He came to teach twelve men, the Apostles, about the process of evolution. The Apostles were preparing to take the first initiation. Jesus was attempting to teach these men about the need to sacrifice the physical, human world in order to achieve in the spiritual world. He wanted them to understand that this sacrifice is best accomplished through service to others. His teaching and his words were engineered to inspire this small group of men to grow spiritually.

Jesus was not the founder of the Catholic club, nor did he intend to influence any religion at all. The Catholics have taken a portion of what Jesus said and added their own absurd nonsense to form the basis of the Catholic religion. On the rare occasions when Catholics do use the actual words of Jesus, they have no idea what those words mean. Words spoken two thousand years ago do not have the same meaning today. It is as though Catholics found someone's personal diary, containing personal messages relevant to only a few people, and used that diary to run their lives by forming a religion. Every week they would gather together to quote phrases from the diary as though this diary had something to do with them.

Because of their own grandiose ideas of self-importance, Catholics believe that Jesus was speaking to them when he was not. In fact, if Jesus were alive today he would not be able to be in close contact with the Catholics. The vibration of the Catholic club and its members is so low that it would be too painful for someone of Jesus' vibration to endure.

In reality, Jesus was born a third degree initiate. This was a rather advanced vibration at that time, given the condition of this planet two thousand years ago. Jesus was a young soul who had achieved his vibration through spiritual ambition rather than through the many thousands of years experience that most souls need in order to accomplish this level of growth. Because of his spiritual ambition he chose that particular lifetime, with his particular mission, to advance himself to the fourth initiation. At that time souls could achieve the fourth initiation only through physical death, and only in a male vehicle. Due to the work and influence of the Brotherhood, these conditions have since changed.

Jesus was attempting to teach a few people about the need for both correct sacrifice and service to others. Jesus served people throughout his life. He actually worked much more directly to help others between the time he was sixteen to age twenty-two than he did during his last three years. His last three years were a time of preparation for his next initiation. As a third degree initiate he had to demonstrate his dedication to spiritual growth.

All third degree initiates undergo some test of power. During this time a person must decide whether to use his or her resources and energies to advance the goals of the human ego, or to use these same resources to advance the spiritual growth of the soul. When Jesus retreated into the desert, he underwent just such a test. He met with the great temptation, at which time a person must distinguish between the false illusions and hopes of the human ego and the real satisfaction and peace achieved only through the soul.

During the last three years of his life, Jesus gathered the Apostles together to teach them about the need for service to others and the importance of sacrificing human ego goals so that the goals of the soul can be met. Most of the Apostles did not understand what he was saying. Some were inspired and were able to take the first initiation. Others, such as Mary Magdalene and Jesus' mother, Mary, were much more inspired to grow than the Apostles. Mary Magdalene is now a fifth degree initiate and Mary is a sixth degree initiate.

People did experience Jesus as "divine." However, Jesus was no more or less the son of God than any soul on this planet. People experience anyone who is four levels of initiation above them as divine. Since most people are uninitiated, fourth degree initiates are experienced as "divine." Some people experience Cory Aquino as divine at the fourth initiation, just as they experienced Jesus as divine. Ghandi was a fourth degree initiate and people experienced him as divine.

People also do not understand anyone who is more than two or three initiations above them. Jesus was grossly misunderstood and misinterpreted, as was Ghandi. They both died at the hands of people who were completely unaware of what these men were trying to do and say.

Jesus did not die the way that he did in order to redeem the Catholics. He died as he did to fulfill his own initiation requirements. He completely understood his own destiny. His death was dramatic partly because he was such a young soul that he still had physical world attachments which could only be broken through such a death. The human part of Jesus was naturally very reluctant and resistant to fulfill this spiritual destiny and to make the necessary sacrifices for his evolution. Through his own spiritual ambition he was able to accomplish an unusual amount of evolution in a single lifetime.

Jesus did not die to save the Catholics. He died to save himself. Crucifixion was not that unusual at the time of his death, and lifespans were very short. In comparison to the lifespans of that time, he was actually old at the age of twenty-five. Catholics view him as a young man who was persecuted and killed. He was actually an old man who completely understood his destiny. Because Catholics have taken Jesus' life out of context and constructed a scheme of religious fantasies around it, they act as though conditions of two thousand years ago were the same as conditions today. The crucifixion of a twenty-five year old man today would be very different than what occurred two thousand years ago. Today such an act would be sensational and extremely newsworthy. However, two thousand years ago it was common practice. Once the Catholics took the life and death of Jesus out of context, they were free to construct any bizarre, self-serving fantasy they wanted to construct.

RITUALS

Since Catholics have completely misinterpreted and distorted Jesus' message of sacrifice and service, their rituals are nothing but the acting out of insane fantasies. Spiritual evolution does require sacrifice but nothing like what the Catholics are doing. Spiritual evolution requires that people sacrifice the goals and objectives of the human ego so that the spiritual goals of the soul can be accomplished. The goals of the human ego usually involve some attempt at success or fulfillment in the human world. People seek high-paying jobs, powerful management positions, or ideal relationships in an attempt to satisfy the human ego. What they cannot see is that the human ego is never satisfied. It always wants more. Spiritual goals involve peace of mind above all else so that the requirements of the planetary initiations can be fulfilled. Sacrificing these human goals is always done on an individual basis, just as spiritual growth is always a function of the individual soul.

Catholics have no interest in individual evolution or with the kinds of sacrifices required to accomplish spiritual growth. Catholics are too preoccupied with their fantasies of personal salvation to grow spiritually. Their rituals of sacrifice promote their fantasies of personal salvation. The Catholic idea of sacrifice is found in the ritual of the Mass. During the Mass, Catholics sacrifice bread and wine on an altar. The priest declares that he has the power to transform this bread and wine into the body and blood of Jesus Christ. This is called the "miracle of transubstantiation of matter."

Once the bread and wine are "transformed," the priest encourages Church members to come forth and eat the flesh and drink the blood of Jesus. What kind of people want to eat flesh and drink blood? What kind of people could possibly believe that such a perverted thing would have anything to do with spiritual growth?

Jesus never said anything about eating flesh or drinking blood. These words were actually spoken by his followers, who were attempting to tell other people what Jesus had taught them. The people the Apostles were attempting to talk to were as barbaric as Hitler's Nazis, only not as violent. The Apostles were attempting to tell these barbarians about the need for the soul and human personality to be fused. They used this language structure because they wanted to deliver this message in a way these primitive barbarians could understand. The Apostles did not understand that they were growing spiritually because they had been inspired by Jesus. None of the Apostles had reached a high enough vibration to be able to pass on the same inspiration or teaching to others.

The Catholics refuse to sacrifice anything that would promote their own evolution. They never sacrifice their painful relationships or human suffering. They do not seek peace of mind or emotional health. They go to Church with all their problems and come home with all the same problems. None of their hurt, suffering or incorrect ideas are ever sacrificed.

Catholics look only for personal salvation. They keep everything in place that prevents evolution. They want absolution for their sins so that they can go out and repeat the same painful behavior patterns without changing their lives. They want plenary indulgences so they can do anything they want with their lives and still be guaranteed "eternal reward." Catholics do not want to sacrifice the idea that they have been saved. Ironically, they are now completely unable to save themselves.

PRIESTS

Catholic priests are attracted to Catholicism because of their own exaggerated ideas about themselves. Priests believe they were called to the priesthood by God. They believe that they have been appointed by God to represent God here on earth. In reality, priests have less connection to God than the people they claim to serve.

Priests are called to the priesthood out of their own damages. Their mission is self-appointed. God, or more accurately the Logos of this planet, is represented by sixth and seventh degree initiates who have achieved a level of spiritual perfection that makes this representation possible. Catholic priests are—with only rare exceptions—uninitiated, which means that their impulses toward physical and emotional abuse are not yet under control. They become priests so that they can act out their personal pathologies through their role as clergy. They use the priesthood to hide from their personal problems, including their inability to relate to other people.

Catholic priests view themselves as above others. They look down on people from their altars. They control and manipulate people through guilt and fear. In actuality, they have helped to destroy the human egos of millions of practicing Catholics to such an extent that these damaged ego structures can no longer perform their proper function as servants to the goals of these souls. Priests like to dress up in robes, jewels and crowns. The Brotherhood asks what kind of men want to parade around in these outfits. Do they think they are little kings or do they like wearing dresses?

Priests are usually born into families with very controlling parents. Their mothers often dominate the home and control the lives of their children. These mothers believe they are good Catholics who have the right to do anything to their children in the name of God. They believe they can control and manipulate the life of another person to fulfill their own religious fantasies. They believe that having a son become a priest is testimony to their personal holiness and a ticket to eternal reward. They see themselves as "Blessed Mothers" who, like Mary the mother of Jesus, are sacrificing their sons for God.

These women are very sick. They have been sickened and driven mad by the Catholic religion. They produce insane sons by rewarding priestly behaviors such as loneliness, isolation, separateness, pride, and arrogance. They discourage healthy, normal sexual relationships and render their sons useless in human relationships. As a result, priests generally are very disturbed people. They suffer from mental illness, alcoholism, and depression more than humanity can imagine. They become involved in homosexual affairs and unhealthy, secret sexual relationships with women. They are lonely and lacking in any real ability to relate. They learn from their parents to ignore their personal problems and to control and manipulate other people's lives.

Priests pretend to be followers of Jesus. They pretend to live as Christ lived and to sacrifice as he sacrificed. This is an absolute lie. Priests have chosen the physical human world, not the spiritual world. In order to grow spiritually a person must sacrifice the human world of comfort, convenience, glamour, power, money, and so forth. Jesus was continually making human world sacrifices. Yet, if people look at priests, no such human world sacrifices are made. In fact, the further a priest moves up the ladder of Catholic hierarchy, the more human power, wealth, glamour and prestige he will gain. The bishops live very luxurious lives. The Pope lives in wealth and splendor while Catholics all over the world are dying each day from starvation. What do these priests think they are sacrificing?

Catholic priests are not followers of Jesus. Jesus was climbing the spiritual ladder of Planetary Hierarchy. Catholic priests are climbing the human ladder of Catholic hierarchy which is more like a downward escalator into darkness. Priests are more interested in reduced clergy air fares and favored treatment in their local restaurants than they are in growing spiritually. They would rather listen to the stories of the sexual "misconduct" of teenage boys in the confessional than to establish healthy, normal human relationships. They are more interested in their collection boxes than in the well-being of the people they claim to serve.

Priests claim to represent God. Yet, if they are so close to God and so connected to God, why can they not heal people? Why are Catholics suffering from so many mental-emotional problems? Why do so many Catholics live in abusive marriages and unhealthy relationships? Why are there so many alcoholics among them? Where are the healing powers of the priests? Jesus healed people.

If priests are like Jesus, why do the Catholics suffer so much human pain and distress?

CATHOLIC EDUCATION

Catholic parents who send their children to parochial schools do so out of their own guilt. They believe they have failed somehow as Catholics. In an attempt to make up for their failures, they vow to make better Catholics out of their children. They think that sending their children to Catholic schools will make their children better Catholics.

These parents cannot see that their religion has failed them. Their religion has failed to provide them with spiritual growth, emotional comfort or mental peace. However, these parents believe they would have found comfort, growth and peace in their religion if only they had been better Catholics. Ironically, they are probably the "best Catholics" this religion could find—they are so burdened with personal guilt they cannot see that the failure is in their religion club and not in them. Since they cannot see that their religion is a failure and a travesty, they send their children to Catholic schools hoping that these children will find the comfort, growth and peace the Catholic club claims to offer.

When children attend any form of current formal education, they are usually severely damaged by the educational system. They do not learn how their desks are made; where pencils come from; what heats their classroom; how books are made; what kinds of wood make up their classroom floors; or how to repair a broken toilet and a leaky faucet. Because education has very little to do with reality, children become disconnected from the real world. They lose all sense of purpose and meaning. Much more will be said about education in the next book from the Brotherhood.

Parochial education offers children even less connection to reality. Catholic education teaches all of the same useless, purposeless subjects taught in public schools, along with all the religious fantasies offered by the Catholic religion club. Parochial school students are not only disconnected from reality but are also filled with frightening, bizarre religious fantasies that only cause more damage and harm.

Catholic schools are usually run by nuns. Catholic nuns, as a group, suffer from very serious psychological disturbances that often prevent them from functioning in normal society. They are protected by their roles as nuns from any challenge that would confront their mental illnesses. These women become nuns because the "sisterhood" allows them to keep their personal problems covered with made-up Catholic fantasies about what they are doing. They become school teachers because the classroom allows them to pass on their disturbances to children through guilt, intimidation, and humiliation.

Catholic nuns are usually raised in strict Catholic families with parents who have little understanding of the real world or of healthy human relationships. Strict Catholic parents know nothing about the individual emotional needs of their children. They are too filled with religious fantasies about good Catholic children and good Catholic parents. They are more interested in raising good Catholics than they are in raising healthy children. Consequently, the more the Catholic parents attempt to be good, strict Catholics, the more emotionally abusive they are with their children.

Good Catholic parents lie to their children about life. They lie to their children about God, and teach them to live in made-up religious fantasy worlds. They raise their children to become irresponsible adults who do not have to work on their problems or do anything about their own evolution.

Catholic nuns simply pass on this pathological parenting to children in the classroom. They frighten children as they were frightened. They humiliate children and teach them to see themselves as failures, just as their own parents did with them. They withhold affection and warmth from children as their own parents did to them. They pass on all their unhealthy attitudes about sex and human relationships which they learned from their own disturbed parents. And they do all this in the name of God, as though passing on their hurt and pain were in some way holy or blessed.

Catholic nuns are as black as the robes that many of them still wear. They are, for the most part, seriously disturbed women who would be placed in psychiatric treatment if they were not hiding out in the convent. Sending a child to a Catholic school is exactly the same as placing that child in the hands of child abusers. Most of these children never recover from their Catholic education. Many of them carry these damages for lifetimes without relief. However, until the parents of these children can face the failure of their own religion, they will continue to allow their children to be abused and harmed in the name of good Catholic education and training.

CATHOLIC WOMEN

Any religion that is truly committed to darkness will suppress and destroy its women. Like Islam and Judaism, the Catholic Church understands that if women were given any form of leadership in the Church the religion would eventually change. Women are more aware of the need to serve others and less damaged by the child-rearing practices that cause men to become power-oriented and dominant. Almost all organizations that provide real service to people are comprised primarily of women.

The Catholic club does not attempt in any way to serve its members, nor does this club want any form of change that would release people from the club's grip of control over their lives. So there are no women priests, bishops or leaders of any kind. Women have no power in the administration of the Church, nor do they have any say in the establishment of Church policy. Instead, the Catholic club is dedicated to destroying its women.

Women are much more serious than men about their religion, particularly in Western societies. Most Catholics hold two very different behavior standards for men and women. Catholic men are told about the rigid rules of the Catholic Church regarding sex, but they are actually taught that "boys will be boys." Catholic women are also taught the same unhealthy, harmful ideas and attitudes about sex. However, the expectation is that women will obey all the made-up Catholic rules about who, when, where, how, and why a person can have sex.

Catholic girls are taught to model their lives after Mary, the mother of Jesus. Mary, to the Catholics, is a statue of a woman dressed in blue and white robes, violently crushing a snake with her foot—which may tell people something about how Catholic women are taught to view sex. Mary was, in reality, a simple, decent woman who understood the spiritual destiny of her son. Her life was difficult but she chose her lifetime with Jesus for the potential spiritual growth that was involved. She was not a martyr, nor was she a saint. She did not conceive Jesus through a cosmic phenomenon. She had normal sexual intercourse like anyone else who conceives a child.

Mary was not an exceptionally holy woman, nor was she unholy. She did not rise up off the earth into a cloud at her death. She died a normal, simple death. She did not sacrifice her life for her son. She used his teaching to inspire her own spiritual growth. Indeed, Mary was so simple, ordinary and human that the Catholics would not recognize her if they were eating dinner with her today. Mary was poor. She lived a meager, shabby life. She was not very intelligent by current standards. Most Catholics today would consider her mentally retarded and undesirable. She would not be welcomed in their homes. Today, she would be more like someone who could be found in a Salvation Army shelter for the poor and homeless.

The Catholics pretend that Mary was a highly evolved soul. She was not. She was not even initiated at the time of Jesus' life. They pretend that Mary was spiritual and holy, and that the way she became so pure was by refraining from sex and enduring emotional pain without attempting to solve her problems. Mary did not refrain from sex nor was she "saintly" when she was faced with normal human pain. Nevertheless, the Catholics impress their made-up lies and fantasies on children from the time they are very young. Anyone who takes Catholicism seriously will have considerable problems with sex and marriage. The women will use glamour and makeup to cover the hatred they feel toward themselves as women. The more makeup they wear and the more self-righteous they act, the more contempt and disdain they have for themselves.

The men will learn to "control" their sexual urges with their wives in order to fulfill their roles as Catholic husbands. At the same time, many will have extramarital affairs with their secretaries, co-workers, and with prostitutes. They will lie about themselves and cheat on their wives because of their Catholic training.

Sex is as natural and healthy for human beings as is food and water. The Catholic club uses sex to control its members through guilt. It is as though the Catholics are saying to their children,

"When you get thirsty, do not take a drink. Only weak, bad people drink when they are thirsty." It is natural for young children to masturbate, just as it is natural for teenagers to have sex. However, when the young children feel the natural urge to masturbate, the Catholic club says, "Do not drink when you are thirsty." Those who do (the majority of them) then feel weak and bad. Even after they "confess" this so-called sin, they still feel bad and guilty. Then, in order to make up for the bad thing they have done, they try to become better Catholics. In the end, all sex becomes wrong in the Catholic consciousness, no matter what the conditions.

Catholic women are taught to see Mary as a victim who suffered her emotional problems silently and without comfort. They believe that to live in human pain is holy. Many think that living with abusive, alcoholic husbands is a saintly act. They believe that to be like Mary is to carry extreme emotional burdens without relief.

Catholic women are trained to think that solving one's problems is sinful and that alleviating one's own psychological burdens is selfish. Because of this they are trapped in so much human pain that it is impossible for them to grow spiritually. They will not sacrifice anything in order to promote their own well-being, and they will cling to hurt and suffering that causes nothing but misery. They will not sacrifice this hurt nor will they sacrifice their own misery. Consequently, all their energies are tied up in protecting their damages. They have no resources left to grow spiritually. They have only their incorrect Catholic ideas and fantasies that keep them powerless and emotionally bankrupt. The Catholic club remains in the hands of the male leaders who protect their self-appointed power at any cost.

THE PAPACY

If humanity could view this planet through the eyes of the Brotherhood, they would see that Rome, Italy appears as an energetic black ball with tentacles reaching throughout the world. The center of this black ball is the center of the Catholic club and its political machine. It represents the darkness of Catholic leadership with its power-hungry, disturbed men.

Catholics pretend that the leadership of the church is divinely inspired. They pretend that their popes represent a long line of spiritual leaders that can be traced back to Saint Peter. In reality, the Pope is elected because of his popularity among the power-hungry cardinals who elect him, and for his political influence in key countries throughout the world. Popes are not chosen because they know anything about evolution or because they care about spiritual growth. They are not chosen for their desire to serve humanity. They are not chosen because of their own spiritual advancement and accomplishment.

Of all the popes who reigned over the Catholic club and were heralded as great spiritual leaders, only three had reached any level of initiation. The fact that these three became popes was purely accidental and had nothing to do with their level of initiation. Pope Pius X was a first degree initiate and also the first initiated pope. It should be said that at the first initiation the soul has only about ten percent spiritual control over the human ego. The first initiation represents a surrendering of only the most basic physical impulses toward war, violence, and greed.

Pope John XXIII was a third degree initiate and the most spiritually advanced of all the popes. John XXIII might best be described as a fledgling third degree initiate. He was very unpopular among his colleagues, who tended to view him as a bumbling fool. Throughout his reign he was under great criticism from the inner ranks, who were completely uninitiated with no ability to recognize any level of spiritual growth whatsoever.

Pope John Paul II is also a first degree initiate. The Brotherhood considers him an advanced first degree initiate because he has done some of the work required for a soul preparing for the second initiation. Even so, he is presently unable to move spiritually because he is so embedded in his own personal pride. This pride is a function of his Polish upbringing and his continued misuse of human will. The net effect is that he is unable to grow spiritually at this time.

All other Catholic popes have been uninitiated. This means that they had no control over the desires and hungers of the human ego. The popes represent a long line of politically-hungry, lost souls attempting to control the lives of other people. They are willing to tell any lies necessary to achieve and maintain that control.

If the Brotherhood were to send spiritual leadership into humanity, those leaders would come only when humanity could listen. They would not be part of a corrupt, organized political machine like the Catholic club. These leaders would each bring accurate, spiritual information to people to help them live healthier, more peaceful lives. True spiritual leaders would not continue repeating the same thing over and over again for centuries without offering any meaning or purpose.

Real spiritual leaders would be dedicated to solving the world problems of hunger and starvation. They would not continue to live in the wealth and pretended royalty of the popes while many of their own people suffered from poverty and pain. Real spiritual leaders would not waste their time parading around in white robes and waving to people along the roadside. Popes want power, wealth and glamour. Real spiritual leaders want humanity lifted out of the unnecessary suffering and pain that people face every day. How can someone claim to be a spiritual leader and do nothing more than wave to starving people in the streets? How can someone claim to be a spiritual leader, allowing himself to be worshiped like an emperor, who has not the slightest bit of genuine hope and comfort for his people? Wearing white robes and gowns cannot cover the reality of the papacy. However, the grandiosity of Catholics, who think they are so important that God has given them spiritual leadership through the popes, is more than enough to blind millions of Catholics to the truth about their leaders.

4

CHRISTIANITY

PERSONAL SALVATION

ALL CHRISTIAN RELIGIONS with a Judeo root are based on the illusion of personal salvation. Between the time of Moses and Jesus, the Jews were busy perfecting the idea of salvation. The reality of spiritual evolution through hard work and sacrifice was too bitter for the Jews. As a group they had been in captivity much too long to face the realities of evolution. They actually did need to be saved from their captors, but such a release would not have caused any evolution. It would only have freed their energies from the cycles of captivity, thus making evolution a possibility.

During this time between Moses and Jesus, the Jews developed their elitist notion that they, the Jews, were the "chosen people." This meant that only by being born a Jew could a soul be "saved." This notion caused the Jews to develop even more "separation" fantasies, and to see themselves as some kind of religious royalty. They decided that through this elitism and separation they could be saved. This decision caused the Jews to view their pathology as the key to eternal salvation.

Jesus came when he did, in part, to confront this idea of elitism and religious royalty. During his life, the Jewish community was divided into those who followed Jesus and those who followed tradition. At the time of Jesus' appearance, it was understood by the Logos that humanity would somehow distort this confrontation that Jesus brought to the idea of personal salvation. It was not known exactly what form this distortion would take.

In 55 A.D. one of the possible distortions emerged. By this time the Dark Side had poisoned and perverted the message of Jesus. Out of these distortions and perversions, the Dark Side gave humanity the Christian symbol of personal salvation—the Cross. At that point, and through all of the centuries following, Christianity used this symbol to completely eradicate all notions of individual evolution, substituting instead the idea of personal salvation. Today the idea of personal salvation is the greatest single barrier to the evolution of humanity.

The symbol of Christian salvation, the Cross or Crucifix, represents violence in the human consciousness. When the human ego looks at a Cross, it registers a violent, gruesome death. When a human figure is draped on the Cross, dripping with blood, the image of violence becomes even more intensified. Because the human ego operates in polarities, it decides that salvation occurs either through violence or through the avoidance of violence. In either polarity, the representation is still one of violence.

In looking at human history, people will see that more wars have been fought in the name of this symbol than for any other single cause during this nearly two thousand year period. More people have died or suffered injuries in wars fought for this symbol than for any other banner or flag. If people would look at the planet even now, they would see war and violence occurring each day in the name of the Cross. When Catholics "bless" themselves by making the sign of the Cross, they are making the sign of violence. They are expressing the idea that purification and salvation can occur through violence. This idea was the underpinning of the Nazi revolution when the Germans, led by Hitler, sought purification and salvation through extreme violence.

All religions formed after 55 A.D. bear the mark of salvation, either from or through violence. All forms of Protestantism, Judaism, Catholicism, Islam, and even Buddhism, have been influenced by the fantasy of salvation. When the Buddhists ask to break from the wheel of life, they are seeking personal salvation rather than individual evolution. The Buddhists, however, have generally managed to refrain from seeking their fantasy salvation through violence.

The Brotherhood cannot impress upon humanity an image that would even begin to describe what has happened to people through the last twenty centuries. They cannot begin to describe the darkness, hurt, and pain that humanity is willing to endure to preserve its beliefs in personal salvation. These conditions have worsened over the last one hundred years. During the nineteenth century, many people had actually begun to carry within themselves the early seeds of discontent with religion. The Brotherhood hoped that these seeds would bear fruit. There was a possibility that people would express their religious discontentment in a way that would begin to lead humanity out of the spiritual slavery caused by fantasies of salvation. Instead, the twentieth century brought to humanity new, advanced technologies, more complicated and abundant information, and glamour. People were besieged by the scientists and their data. They became mesmerized by excitement and sensationalism. In the face of all the confusion and change, humanity retreated back into religious ideas and fantasies, because these offered the only refuge they could find. Humanity was simply too damaged and too endarkened to seek the real refuge and peace that can only be found through spiritual evolution. As a result, humanity is now spiritually paralyzed. None of the Western religion clubs have the ability to offer any relief for this paralysis. In fact, all these religion clubs can do is further cripple and damage people by keeping them drugged on religious cliches so that none of the real problems ever get solved.

Now, the Brotherhood returns to the outer world to help humanity. The Brotherhood offers humanity a healing technology that alleviates human suffering and promotes evolution. (The specifics of this technology can be found in Chapter Eight.) Yet, people are so convinced they have been saved that they do not believe they have to do anything for their evolution. It is impossible for the Brotherhood to teach people about individual evolution when so much of humanity's energy is tied up in the fantasy of salvation.

Most people who received the healing instruments described in the Introduction of this book refused to hold them as directed, for even a few minutes each day. Over the past four years, thousands of these instruments have been distributed to people. Because this project is offered by the Brotherhood as a service to humanity, no one has been charged a fee. The work functions strictly on the basis of donations and has been made available to anyone who requests aid. Of the people requesting instruments, thousands have received help and are consciously aware of the positive effects of the healing instruments. Yet, only a handful have caught on to the idea of evolution. Very few have passed the healing instruments along to other people, or made any attempt to use the energetic resources made available to them for spiritual growth. Most people have simply slipped back into spiritual passivity and inertia, and into the certainty that they have already been saved.

There is no evidence to point to personal salvation. The idea that someone could live only a single lifetime is an infantile idea. The evidence in reality supports evolution, but it is so obvious that people cannot see it. You are much smarter now than you were ten years ago. Ten years from now, you will be even smarter. Ten lifetimes from now, you will be even smarter.

Personal salvation assumes that a child who is born in the ghetto will have the same opportunities as people who are born into wealth. Most ghetto teenagers can tell you that this is not true. People need many lifetimes to accumulate enough experiences to produce spiritual growth. They need to have the experiences of poverty and wealth, of royalty and of unimportance, of maleness and femaleness, and so forth, in order to gather information about reality. All of this could, in theory, be done in one lifetime but most souls would find it impossible under current conditions. Even under ideal conditions, souls need time to acquire the many experiences that are needed to accomplish spiritual evolution.

THE BIBLE

We have already discussed how people have concluded that the Bible contains accurate spiritual information, and how this false conclusion prevents people from discovering the actual reality of spiritual evolution. We would say that the Bible is currently the single greatest barrier to humanity's spiritual understanding. Agreement among people is very strong and not easily shaken, despite the overwhelming evidence that the Bible is not a spiritual guidebook. About ten percent of the Bible is actually inspired writing. Inspired writing means that a person in the outer physical world was able to write down information that was telepathically communicated from the Brotherhood, who exist in the Inner World. The Ten Commandments, for example, was inspired writing. Moses did not go to the top of a mountain and see a ball of fire come from the sky to write the Ten Commandments on two stone tablets. The information was telepathically communicated to Moses from a fourth degree initiate. Moses then wrote the Commandments in a way that he and his followers could understand.

Many people who wrote parts of the Bible thought they were hearing voices that were somehow divine or inspired. Some people were, in fact, hearing voices. These voices, however, were not coming from the Brotherhood, but rather from souls located on the lower astral planes. There are many planes of existence beyond earth. The astral planes are places between earth and the Summerland which souls must pass through at death. Some souls pass through these planes, shedding the human personality traits, without difficulty. Others get caught in these places for thousands of years. Many are caught because they are insistent that their religious fantasies of heaven be fulfilled. They refuse to listen to the Brotherhood or to accept the aid that is being offered to them. They are like prisoners, only they are not in cells. Most psychics obtain their information from souls on the astral planes. These souls are caught in these planes because they know nothing about spiritual evolution. Out of ignorance they refuse the help of the Brotherhood. They seek, instead, to influence other people's lives and interfere where they do not belong.

Information received from these souls is never divine or inspired. It is useless and often inaccurate, and when accepted as divine it is gibberish. Most psychics and "inspired" writers today who think they are receiving divine information are listening to the mumblings of confused astral entities.

The inspired portion of the Bible was written for very specific groups of people at particular times in history. These teachings had meaning only for those people for whom they were intended.

Reading these passages today would be like listening to a speech given by Roosevelt in the 1930s or Kennedy in the 1960s and trying to divine meaning and inspiration from these speeches. Information given in the 1930s would not be relevant to the 1960s, nor would information given in the 1960s mean the same thing in the 1980s.

Most of the Bible, in fact ninety percent of it, is nothing more than fragmented gibberish. Each person who wrote about Jesus, for instance, had a completely different experience of him. Some who wrote never met him. They were writing down what they thought they heard about him. Much of what the Bible contains was written by people with inferior mental vehicles who were attempting to communicate to other people with similar inferior vehicles. When Moses wrote the Ten Commandments he was trying to communicate with the Hebrews. By today's standards of intelligence, the average I.Q. of the Hebrews ranged from sixty-two to sixty-four.

Even if people could sort out the ten percent of inspired information contained within the Bible, it would be of little use. First, it would be impossible to evaluate the inspired information without having telepathic rapport with the Brotherhood. Such rapport could only be established by reaching certain levels of evolution. People who read the Bible are not evolving, so the likelihood of establishing such communication would be nearly impossible.

Secondly, there would only be a few sections of the Bible relevant to people today. And these few sections would only cause inspiration in a person if the writings were read at certain strategic times in a person's evolution, which could also only be determined by telepathic rapport with the Brotherhood.

Simply said, the Bible is—for the most part—of no spiritual value. If ten percent of a person's diet is healthy, nourishing food and ninety percent of the diet is garbage, that person will be poisoned by the garbage. Reading the Bible poisons the consciousness with inaccurate information and fragmented gibberish that have nothing to do with the reality of spiritual evolution.

Only about one percent of the information found in the Bible is relevant to spiritual evolution. If people were able to compile all the information which is needed by souls to accomplish spiritual growth, they would find this information very contradictory. It would be specific information pertaining only to certain souls at certain times, and it would not be understood by anyone else. For example, if someone eats too much, that person would need to be told to eat less. If someone eats too little, that person would need to be told to eat more. So it is with souls. Some souls need a personal privacy, while others need to live in large families. Some souls need to establish personal independence, while others require more protected, dependent life situations. Rarely are souls born into families where they can actually be provided with what they need. So even if people did find accurate spiritual information somewhere, they would not only find it contradictory, but they would probably conclude that it was inaccurate as well.

Jesus did inspire people to grow spiritually, but not with meaningless, fragmented, linear commands. Such inspiration is not found in the flat, linear world of the human mind. When children are asked to read the Bible or told Bible stories, they are bored and annoyed. When adults listen to Sunday sermons about the Bible, they are bored also. They are not inspired to lead healthier lives. They are not inspired to give up the things in their lives that cause them pain in favor of a spiritual path. They are not encouraged to seek peace of mind or a higher state of consciousness. They are only further cemented into their incorrect ideas and empty fantasies about life.

When people read the Bible or listen to a sermon, they are not uplifted or redirected in a more positive way. In fact, most people are bored or drugged on the religious cliches. They do not imagine themselves in an ongoing process of change and evolution. The Bible does not stir the imagination or arouse creative thought. The Bible is a flat, linear, dead book filled with fragmented gibberish. Using the Bible as a guide to living makes for a flat, linear, going-nowhere existence. It is a book for people who want to stay the same and remain endarkened in the human world, guided only by made-up human ideas.

People who read the Bible should know that they would get as much spiritual information from the Bible as they would from reciting passages out of a 1953 Chevy repair manual. In fact, they would actually learn more about reality from the Chevy manual than they would from the Bible. The automobile manual is not mindless gibberish, and actually contains information that can be used to set something aright in the physical world. The Bible does not teach anything about the physical world, nor does it tell people how to set their lives aright.

It is both ludicrous and sad to see people reading the Bible who are much more advanced than the people who wrote it. The mental vehicles today are far more developed than they were two thousand years ago. Some of today's Christians are first and second degree initiates who are much more spiritually advanced than the Apostles were at that time. These people are even more spiritually advanced than the ministers and priests they try to follow. Some initiates discover this but continue to follow their ministers, priests, and Bibles. This actually causes them to lose their spiritual vibration and to move backward rather than forward.

PROTESTANT CLUBS

Over the centuries that followed the life of Jesus, the Catholic club gained a world-wide political power base. The popes were acting like self-proclaimed dictators who attempted to control matters of both church and state. The early Protestants did not want this kind of interference from the Pope. They were political leaders themselves who wanted to remain in political power. They were also ruthless hedonists who wanted to have their sexual freedom without papal intervention. These early Protestants were not protesting against the darkness of the Catholic Church as much as they were protesting the popes' political interferences and doctrines on sex and marriage. Because the early Protestants wanted political power and sexual freedom, they established various forms of Protestantism that would meet their political and personal needs. As a result, Protestantism tends to be less rigid in its rules and regulations than Catholicism, and therefore less damaging to people on the whole.

Although Protestantism is inclined to be less damaging, this does not mean that any Protestant religion offers a spiritual path. Protestants are enslaved by their beliefs in personal salvation just like the Catholics and the Jews. All forms of Protestantism are born out of the human world and therefore have no spiritual value. Protestantism only tends to be less damaging because it places less emphasis on manipulating people through fear and guilt, and more emphasis on the individual interpretation of the Bible. This allows each Protestant sect and each individual church member to interpret the Bible in whatever way promotes their political aspirations or personal sexual preferences.

The focus of most Protestant rituals is prayer and song rather than dogma and doctrine. Again, neither prayer nor song will produce positive spiritual results, but neither damages the human ego structure in the same way that Catholicism and Judaism damage the consciousness. In fact, the latter tend to damage the human ego structure beyond repair, even with the use of the technology now offered to humanity by the Brotherhood.

The least harmful forms of Protestantism can be found among black Protestant congregations. In these communities Sunday services are much more like uplifting song fests than religious meetings. Black people in Western society generally have much healthier attitudes toward religion than white people of any religious denomination.

Protestantism would have been even less destructive to humanity if the original founders had been able to be more honest about their desires for political power and sexual freedom. However, they were not honest, but were instead righteous. As a result, Protestant ministers tend to be very righteous, and the Protestant clubs tend to arouse righteousness in their members. Protestants think that righteousness is holy. They like rousing sermons by self-righteous ministers. They think that the more one can experience righteousness, the more spiritual one becomes. They do not see that the more righteous one becomes, the more insane one becomes. Righteousness causes disturbances in people's thinking and in their ability to relate to others. Protestant clubs that seek righteousness are seeking a path of mental-emotional destruction. Unfortunately, no one will be able to stop them. Their righteousness has become so positive and certain that it is impossible to challenge their beliefs. When this righteousness is confronted by reality, it is only met with more righteousness. Since this book is about reality, most Protestant club members who read it will respond with righteousness.

Protestants claim that spiritual growth can be accomplished through the Bible. Since Protestantism offers unlimited interpretations of the Bible, and the Bible is nothing but gibberish, Protestantism is the mental junkyard religion. Protestantism is like a dump site that is big enough to contain all the trash accumulated in a week in all five boroughs of New York City. Each Protestant sect drives up to the site and fills up with mental garbage and trash, and then drives away. Each group pretends that these "treasures" give them peace of mind and comfort in troubled times. Everyone has faith that what is in the truck is not trash. Every Sunday the minister gives out the junk. He or she gives each person a bag full of mental trash. Then, the truck is taken back to the dump for another haul.

Human interpretations of religious gibberish are trash. The mental trash that Protestantism offers people does not give them comfort or peace of mind. The self-righteousness inherent in Protestantism prevents people from recognizing the fact that they have been given a bag of trash. When people accumulate enough mental trash, their view of reality becomes completely poisoned.

MINISTERS

Protestant ministers, like rabbis and priests, are attracted to the ministry because they want power and control over people's lives. Protestantism, particularly, attracts ministers who are dedicated to righteousness and glamour, not evolution. There are two kinds of ministers—the ambitious ones and the unambitious ones. The ambitious ministers seek large audiences in order to fulfill their ambitions. They are the televangelists and ministers-turned-politicians who want to stand up before thousands of people and shout righteous cliches. These religious leaders are not likely to be able to sit and listen to an individual's problems because to listen to one person is not ambitious enough for these types. They are usually too sick and righteous to have a normal conversation. They use all of their resources to fulfill their ambition for power, and cannot feel powerful by tending to one lost sheep in a possible herd of thousands. As well-meaning as some of these religious leaders may be, they can only reflect their own problems of righteousness and hunger for power because they are too unevolved to have any connection to the Brotherhood or the Logos of this planet. Ironically, if the ambitious ones actually understood evolution, they could use the same ambition that now drives them to achieve power to accomplish spiritual evolution. If any of these people decided to grow spiritually, the rest of the world would not recognize them. They would begin to demonstrate more than just constant righteousness. The energy that is now trapped in the single quality of righteousness would be used to fill in those aspects of the minister's consciousness that are now being robbed by his or her ambitions and dedication to righteousness. People would experience less and less of their ministers' ambitious human personalities and would quickly lose interest in them.

People want their religious leaders to be righteous. They want them to be ambitious in the human world. Unfortunately, people are now destined to get what they want. They can be assured that, in addition to the present televangelists, there are many more righteous souls who are not yet in incarnation. These other souls have been reincarnating into the same religious roles for hundreds and thousands of years. In fact, the ones who will come will be far more righteous than today's evangelists, and much more disturbed. They will continue to come until humanity seeks something better.

The ambitious ministers also tend to be competitive with one another. They swing between the hard line (which is the hell, fire and damnation approach) and the soft line (which is that people are already saved because Jesus loves everyone no matter what they have done). When too many ministers are preaching the hard line, the competitive ones swing into the soft line. When people get tired of the soft line, the ambitious ministers then swing back into the hard line. None of them can see that to be damned or to be saved means the same thing to the human consciousness. In either case, the person listening is invited into passivity. If a person is damned, there is nothing that the person *can* do. If a person is saved, then there is nothing the person *needs* to do. Neither approach produces any evolution.

The unambitious ministers are more likely to tend to the needs of the individual. However, this does not imply that they would provide a person with any kind of real help or relief. Ministers, even the unambitious ones, want power and control over people's lives. They speak of their fears of hell and pray that the devil will stay away. As long as they pretend that the devil is outside of them, they live in a world of darkness and fantasy. Another term for the devil might be the human ego. The human ego has completely lost sight of its only intended function, which is to serve the purpose of the soul. The devil is that aspect of the human ego that robs the soul of energy and life force so that it can carry out its own human goals without regard for the soul. The devil is the thief within the human ego structure that uses the person's life to become powerful, successful, famous, comfortable, secure, stable, and wealthy in the human world. The Dark Side has no need to work to keep any devils alive. Human egos all over this planet are automatically doing the devil's work, which is always to rob the soul and prevent spiritual evolution.

Since ninety-eight to ninety-nine percent of this planet is uninitiated, most Protestant ministers are acting completely out of darkness without any guidance from their souls. They want power and control only. They do not want spiritual growth. They like the power they feel when they speak from the podium. Some like the excitement and glamour that their roles as ministers offer to them. They like the image of the "good and righteous" minister and his family because it fulfills old parental ideas and expectations.

They like these things enough to lie about their ability to heal people and their calling to serve them. They like power enough to fill Church members with made-up trash about God and salvation that has nothing to do with the spiritual evolution of this planet.

Some ambitious ministers have amassed great power and wealth in the name of Jesus. They drive expensive cars, own elaborate mansions, and wear glamourous suits and clothes. They claim that they are being led by Jesus. If Jesus were alive today he would not be driving a $25,000 car, nor would he be wearing a $500 suit. Jesus was an ordinary man. Spiritually advanced souls are always very ordinary. If Jesus were alive today, he would be driving a very used car and he would probably wear second-hand clothes. He would be lucky if he could get a dozen people to listen to him. He would not have his own television show and he would not be running for President. He would not be taking money from people to enhance his own personal life. Jesus would not be standing up in front of millions of people admonishing them not to satisfy their senses, while bringing extreme sense satisfaction to himself through the very act of sermonizing. He would not perform "healing" services in front of cameras like a cheap circus act. He would be trying to do something to help people that was real and honest. If Jesus were alive today, he would not be able to be near any well-known minister of any sect. These ministers would all be too dark and dishonest to get near Jesus or any other real spiritual leader.

The Brotherhood asks those who claim to heal and comfort in the name of Jesus to come forth and test their powers. The Brotherhood suggests that these ministers find schizophrenics and depressed people and "heal" them. Find people with chronic headaches, backaches, and other "stress" illnesses and "heal" them. Find people suffering from the emotional losses of death or divorce and "heal" them. Use your platitudes and prayers. Then, the Brotherhood will provide their technology offered through Gentle Wind. Let humanity judge who are the charlatans and fakes, and who has the real connection to God.

THE PROTESTANT ETHIC

The Protestant Ethic refers to the idea that hard work leads to eternal reward. Eternal reward in the human consciousness refers to personal salvation. The hard work that Protestants propose is not the hard work of personal evolution but rather the hard work necessary to achieve human success.

Protestants, like Catholics, are convinced that Jesus died on the Cross at Calvary to redeem them. Protestants, like Catholics, have completely missed the fact that Jesus was attempting to demonstrate the difficulty of spiritual evolution. Jesus showed people that evolution requires many personal sacrifices—sacrifices that Protestants feel no need to make.

When Protestants refer to the Protestant Ethic, they are really saying that they already have salvation so they can now work hard at achieving anything they want in the physical human world and not be held responsible for those activities in any way. They are saying that working hard to achieve in the human world is sacred and spiritual, and pleasing to their illusion of God.

The fantasy of the Protestant Ethic allows Protestants to work hard at fulfilling human goals, not spiritual goals. It encourages

people to become top notch executives and successful profession-
als, to earn comfortable salaries and to live in their dream homes
as though these human goals were in some way spiritual and correct. In fact, the Protestant Ethic encourages Protestants to seek
all forms of human success and comfort, as if success and comfort
would produce spiritual growth.

This is exactly the opposite of spiritual reality. The Age of Darkness has left humanity without spiritual direction. People run their
lives completely from the human ego, seeking to fulfill human
goals. The human ego, by its nature, wants to find a comfortable,
stable, easy way to live. The human ego wants to keep things the
same. It wants to move into its dream house with its dream family,
drive around in its dream car and earn a good salary at its dream
job. It wants to do the same thing in the same way every day. The
"Protestant Ethic" allows people to fool themselves into believing
that this is what good people do with their lives, and that as good
people they will find their reward at death.

Evolution is a process of growth that requires continuous, ongoing change. In order for a soul to grow, constant change is required. These evolutionary changes are always engineered and
directed by the soul, not the human ego. Evolution is a process of
giving up personal, human preferences in favor of spiritual goals.
If a person does find comfort and stability in a dream home and
dream family, the soul cannot grow. Comfortable people, in fact,
have the least opportunity for evolution because they do not want
to change anything. People only want to change things in their
lives when they are in emotional pain and discomfort. Ironically,
comfortable people are often more capable of growing because they
are not burdened with serious mental-emotional problems. Unfortunately, they are just too attached to what they would call "the
good life."

Human comfort is spiritually deadly. The Age of Darkness has
made this comfort appear inviting, and the Protestant Ethic makes
it seem spiritually correct. Evolution is continuous movement upward through the seven planetary initiations. When souls are
evolving, they cannot afford to stop and plant roots in human
comfort. They must seek spiritual comfort—which is not available
through Protestantism or any other religion that offers the fantasy
of salvation.

It is ironic that this idea that human hard work can reap eternal reward has been called an "ethic." This illusion leads to extremely unethical behaviors. This illusion allows people to think that climbing to the top of the executive ladder is spiritual, no matter how they get there or why they are climbing in the first place. It allows Protestant and "Christian" businessmen and women to treat their employees any way they want, to live in devastating marriage relationships, to emotionally abuse their children, and to ignore their personal problems as well as those of their neighbors. They may conduct their lives in this way without doing anything to change themselves, as long as they attend Church services and activities when such attendance is convenient. These people are unethical and irresponsible, but they are considered good Christians, good Protestants. If they had any idea why they were alive and what they came here to do, they would be horrified at what they have created out of their lives.

BORN AGAIN CHRISTIANS

Of all the current forms of Christianity, the Born Again Christians, along with the Charismatics and Jehovah's Witnesses, are the most extreme and seriously disturbed. Born Again Christians have not been "born again" in any way. They are usually people who "find" religion in a time of personal crisis such as divorce, illness, a death, or some more serious mental-emotional problem. When the crisis passes they feel better. They then associate their new religion with the relieved condition or feeling of improvement, and claim that they have been "born again."

In reality, they feel better because the crisis has passed, not because of anything that has happened through their religion. People do not understand that problems change over time no matter what they do. Many people who attend psychotherapy think that their therapy is causing them to feel better. Most people who attend psychotherapy sessions would have felt better even if they had spent the hour in the grocery store or in the bathtub.

When people participate in religion clubs such as the Born Again Christians, they continually credit their religion with things that the religion is simply not able to do. This means that they lose the basic relationship between cause and effect, or that they have failed to make a proper connection between cause and effect. Because they cannot see that their religion has not caused their relief or improved feeling, they over-invest in their religion. In fact, whenever people fail to make the appropriate connection between cause and effect, they misdirect their energies into the wrong things.

Born Again Christians invest their energies and resources into a religious fantasy life. The more they do so, the more disconnected from reality they become. As they disconnect from actual reality, they become mentally and emotionally ill, and less able to manage themselves in the physical world.

The more that Born Again Christians invest in their religious fantasies, the less energy they have to solve their real problems. This is true for anyone of any religion. The more energy the religion takes from the person, the less that person is able to solve his or her real problems. When people do not have the energy and resources to solve their personal problems, they become unable to grow spiritually. Their lives become a world of mental ideas and illusions which quickly destroy any remaining emotional stability.

Becoming a "Born Again" Christian is a romantic idea to some people. They experience their new religion the same way some people experience "falling in love." They do not see that "falling in love" (which most people never really experience) is more like falling into fantasies about love that have nothing to do with the reality of human relationships. They also do not see that it is very easy for people to invest their energies in their relationship fantasies, but painfully difficult to divest their energies from relationships they no longer want. It is much easier for most people to get married than it is for them to get divorced.

Those people who think that becoming a Born Again Christian is a romantic idea do not understand how difficult it is to divorce one's energies from religious fantasies once they are invested. They do not see how dangerous their investment actually is. They do not understand that the moment they give credit to their religion for something their religion simply did not do, they reset the course of their lives on a path of personal destruction. Once they invest in religious fantasies instead of reality, they begin to sacrifice their mental-emotional health and all possibility of spiritual growth.

The only way that course can then be altered is through the discovery that their religion has failed them completely. Even when people make this discovery, they usually cover it up immediately with another religious fantasy. They automatically protect their energetic investment by making another bad investment.

As a result, most Born Again Christians are too damaged to grow spiritually, and will need hundreds of years to unravel the damage. Most of these people really become lost souls, which is much worse than the original crisis that caused them to seek "God." The more vehement they are about their religion, the more spiritually lost they are. The more invested they are in the religion, the more sick they become. The more "faith" they have, the less likely they are to recover from their misdirected course without many lifetimes of pain and suffering that religious fantasies will not temper.

Again, we should note that most of the above refers only to Born Again Christians who are also Caucasian. Black people in Western societies generally do not use religion in the same way that white people do. As a group, they have been too preoccupied fighting for basic human rights and survival to have the energy to invest in religious fantasies. Their energies have been so desperately needed in other areas that they could not afford the luxury of entertaining constant religious illusions and lies. They have instead used their religions as a focal meeting point for their dilemma as a people. They have used it for singing and for generating a feeling of camaraderie in their plight, and have therefore generally avoided the serious damage that whites have incurred through their membership in religious duties. Blacks, however, are equally burdened by the fantasy of personal salvation inherent in all religions, and have no more spiritual growth occurring than do whites.

CHARISMATICS AND JEHOVAH'S WITNESSES

The Charismatics, like the Born Again Christians, are drawn to these groups because of some serious personal crisis. Like the Born Again Christians, the Charismatics and Jehovah's Witnesses credit their religions with relief and improvement that these religions simply do not provide. People who join and follow these groups have lost the connection between cause and effect. Consequently, like the Born Again Christians, they then invest their energies in religious fantasies and set their lives on a course of mental-emotional destruction.

The Charismatics, however, get sick even faster than other Christian groups because they have developed a group system or game for passing off damages to one another. The game might best be called "it." "It" is usually the newest member of the group because new members are the most vulnerable. They are vulnerable because they are usually involved in some mental-emotional crisis that has caused them to seek the "help" of the Charismatic group. The game is played much like the game of psychotherapy. In psychotherapy, the patient seeks the help of a psychotherapist because of some emotional problem. The psychotherapist pretends to offer help and advice. In reality, the psychotherapist has been trained—usually in a graduate school program—to manipulate and control people through his or her own damages. In the process of offering "help," the psychotherapist passes off these damages onto the patient. In this way the therapist can continue to protect his or her own pain and problems (which are usually much worse than any of the patients' problems) by passing off the hurt and pain onto people who are vulnerable and in need of real help.

Charismatic groups operate the same way. Group members pretend to be helping one another. They pretend to offer help and support which they are incapable of providing because they are all so sick mentally and emotionally. "It" is the person who needs the most help and is therefore vulnerable enough to accept other people's unresolved hurts and damages. As long as group members have an "it" everyone feels better. They feel better because, like psychotherapists, they are continuously passing off their hurt onto someone else. In this system, no one gets better. Everyone keeps their own problems but uses the other group members to prevent having to experience the pain inherent in those problems. The problems never get solved; the pain merely gets passed off to someone more vulnerable.

Charismatics need many meetings and contacts with other members so they can keep the pain of their own problems away from themselves. The more invested a person is in the Charismatic movement, the more sick the person is, because the investment equals the amount of unresolved personal pain. "It" is a tragic and deadly psychological game because no one gets better. All of a person's resources and energies are tied up in passing off personal damage. Charismatics live like drug addicts who need a fix or an "it" so they do not have to feel the pain of reality.

Some Charismatics believe they are hearing divine voices. Many of these "voices" are nothing but mental echoes that exist only in their own minds. These echoes develop because these people are disturbed, and because they insist on living in made-up religious fantasy worlds. Others who claim to hear voices have connected up with souls on the lower astral planes. These souls are usually caught in these places because of their own damage and ignorance. As previously mentioned, listening to the voices of these souls is like taking personal advice from criminals and back ward psychiatric patients. They offer nothing but confusion, chaos, and disturbance, and have nothing to do with anything that is divine or spiritual.

Because Charismatics are never able to solve their personal problems, they are completely unable to grow spiritually. They have no resources available to look at their lives and to actually solve the problems that brought them to the religion in the first place. They are as preoccupied with passing off their damages as heroin addicts who need a fix. They are as desperate as street junkies to avoid personal pain and they are operating from exactly the same ego system. The only difference is that the heroin addicts are more honest about what they are doing.

The Charismatics, Born Again Christians, and Jehovah's Witnesses all attract sick, fanatical people. These groups, of all the Christian groups, are the most anxious to recruit new members. The Charismatics need new members to keep the game going. The Jehovah's Witnesses, however, seek to spread the "word" as they call it because their idea of the "word" is so far off course. They are the ones who will actually knock on doors and attempt to recruit members. The reason they do so is because the more off course a person gets, the more he or she tries to take other people along. The Jehovah's Witnesses have strayed very far away from the path of evolution. They have wandered so far into their religious fantasy worlds that they cannot get back. All they can do is try to take others with them. The more inaccurate a religion becomes, the more anxious its members are to spread that religion.

The Jehovah's Witnesses have strayed farther than most other Christian groups and are therefore the most preoccupied with getting other people to go along for the ride.

THE POWER OF THE PULPIT

Power, in the human world, is always a function of opposition. In order for a person to become a president or head of any country, there must be active opposition to that person's views or beliefs. Adolph Hitler rose to power because he was able to incite enormous opposition to his disturbed political ideas. Khomeini rose to power in Iran in the same way. Neither of these men were popular with their own people. They were too disturbed and sick to be popular. However, they were vehemently opposed, which more than fueled their political positions.

Ronald Reagan was elected because no one wanted a movie star to become president. He verbally opposed all the things for which the democratic party claimed to be working. Jimmy Carter, on the other hand, had very little opposition and therefore wielded very little power. Carter was flat while Reagan was energized. In the same way, George McGovern lost to Richard Nixon because McGovern could not mount enough opposition to his own views. McGovern could not get the Ku Klux Klan, the Right-to-Lifers, Pro-Choice, or any controversial group to speak out actively against him. His campaign had no opposition, while people clearly opposed Richard Nixon. Many Americans were shocked to discover that a man with Richard Nixon's views could become president over a man with George McGovern's views.

It should be noted here that a person's views do not necessarily have anything to do with how that man or woman will act once elected to office. Ronald Reagan is a perfect example of a staunch right-wing, pro-business republican in his views. Yet, he is a liberal democrat in many of his policies. This discrepancy between beliefs and actions will be discussed in a future book on education. Here, We only wish to emphasize that as Reagan has done more popular things—such as tax reform—he has lost some of his opposition, and therefore his power. He had begun to lose power long before the Iran incident occurred.

In the same way, for ministers to obtain power they must incite opposition to their position. Almost all of the televangelists' sermons are designed to incite opposition, whether that opposition is real or fabricated. The fastest way to incite fabricated opposition is to use the idea of the devil, and of non-believers doing the work of the devil. Televangelists speak out often against the work of the devil, and incite their people into believing strongly in this opposition to what is "good." It is the energetic investment that people make against the devil that brings power to the minister.

Many ministers then claim that they need many millions of dollars to build hospitals, schools, or other institutions that will fight the devil. In reality, they are amassing personal fortunes in the name of some cause that must be fought against the devil. When their followers give money, they do so because they have been led to believe that they are fighting the opposition (the devil) through their financial gifts. Not many ministers would be able to enlist financial support to buy themselves expensive homes, cars, clothes, and other material acquisitions if they had no opposition. People would not do the things that ministers tell them to do if they did not believe these actions were helping to fight the devil.

When the televangelists claim that they are working for the hungry or the homeless, these claims are only partially true. These so-called evangelists may be giving money to help the homeless and hungry, but they are only doing so to cover their real game— which is power, fame, wealth, and glamour. People who are truly working to help the hungry are not buying weekly television time to give sermons. They are not wearing five-hundred-dollar suits or collecting expensive horses. They are just serving humanity. They do not have any power because they have not incited any opposition. The ministers, on the other hand, want personal power more than they want anything else. If these ministers were actually able to convince everyone that their way was correct, there would be no more "bad people" and no one would be doing the devil's work. There would be no opposition and, therefore, they would have no power. Fortunately for them, there is an endless supply of "devil" fantasies to conjure up, and therefore their positions of power through righteousness against the devil remain unchallenged.

PRAYING TO JESUS

Many Christians claim to have found a friend in Jesus. They claim that Jesus speaks to them and answers their prayers. Jesus is much too busy serving the Logos of this planet to be offering friendship to people who know nothing of what it means to have or to be a friend. When people pray and talk to Jesus they are talking to an imaginary friend in the same way that lonely children make up imaginary friends and playmates. Lonely children tell their imaginary friends about their thoughts, feelings, and problems because they have no one they can safely relate to in their everyday lives.

Christians talk to Jesus because they have no one in reality who will listen to them. They are like lonely children who are unable to go out into the world and establish real relationships. Sometimes the Christians talk to their imaginary friend, Jesus, when they are alone. Sometimes they talk to their friend in groups and at prayer meetings. When they talk to Jesus at prayer meetings, they are all talking to the same imaginary friend out of the same isolated, lonely place inside of themselves.

Many Christians claim that Jesus talks to them and answers their prayers. They are actually hearing the echoes of their own minds in the same way that children hear responses from their fantasy playmates. These mental echoes are comforting to people who have no real friends. The idea of having an imaginary playmate is a very comforting idea, especially to an alienated child.

Because Christians have strayed so far off the evolutionary track, they cannot see how ludicrous it is to think that Jesus spends his time catering to the whims of so-called human prayer.

Human fantasies about Jesus are exactly like human fantasies about Santa Claus. The fantasy of Santa is a group fantasy that developed from a real character who was not anything like the present-day fantasy portrayed of Santa Claus. Everyone agrees that today's fantasy Santa acts and dresses a certain way. No one pretends that Santa has dark brown hair, wears Anderson-Little slacks and sweaters, and drives a Subaru station wagon.

The fantasy of Jesus is also a group fantasy that developed from a real person who was unlike anything portrayed today. Everyone agrees that the fantasy Jesus thinks and acts in certain ways. These fantasy ways have nothing to do with the spiritual reality of Jesus; they only serve the needs of lonely, friendless people. In reality, Jesus is doing a lot more to serve humanity than the Christians could possibly imagine. However, he is not in the business of answering their whims. Nor is any other evolved soul interested in human whims and needs in any way that Christians would understand. Jesus is not in the business of offering friendship to anyone. He is doing something much better than that. Sadly, the Christians cannot even begin to comprehend spiritual reality, and are content to be satisfied with the petty comfort offered by an imaginary playmate whom they call Jesus.

5

ISLAM, COMMUNISM & SUFISM

ISLAM, THE RELIGION of the Middle East, has found its way to many other parts of the world. Muslims, the followers of Islam, believe they are guided by the teachings of Muhammad and that they are following Muhammad's way. Like the Christians who misinterpreted and distorted the life of Jesus, the Muslims have misinterpreted and distorted the life of Muhammad. The members of the Islam club are not following the spiritual way of Muhammad; they are following the fanaticism of disturbed Islamic political leaders who represent darkness, violence, and chaos.

Between the sixth and seventh centuries, Muhammad arose as a spiritual leader in a small section of the Arab world. Like Jesus, Muhammad incarnated to fulfill a specific spiritual mission. Like Jesus, the mission was directly related to his own spiritual growth. If Muslims were actually following in the footsteps of Muhammad, they too would be interested in fulfilling the requirements necessary for spiritual growth. Muslims have no such interests. They are completely focused on meaningless Islamic religious rituals.

They are not growing spiritually and have not grown spiritually since Muhammad's death.

Like Jesus of Nazareth, Muhammad had a specific message that was meant only for a specific group of people. These people were primarily tribesmen who were living without any respect for themselves or one another. These people were thieves, rapists, murderers and cutthroats. Their lives were completely out of control. They thought nothing of stealing from one another or causing physical harm when their emotions ran rampant. The men of these tribes mistreated their wives and ignored their female children. They were at war with other neighboring communities. They had no peace and no purpose. They were of a very low vibration, lacking all notion of good will and brotherhood.

Muhammad's teachings were offered to humanity by the Brotherhood. Muhammad was a second degree initiate who came to help a small group of people learn to control their abusive, violent behaviors. He attempted to use the language structure and symbols that would best teach the simple notion of respect and devotion. Devotion is a necessary lesson for all potential first degree initiates. Devotion has to do with gaining enough respect for oneself and others to become capable of listening to someone who knows more about life. Unless a person has accomplished the ability to listen to and follow the directions of a teacher, that person cannot grow spiritually. He or she is simply unable to obtain the necessary information and assistance to accomplish growth.

Muhammad's mission was simple but very difficult. He was asked to become a sort of parent figure to a group of hostile, violent adults who needed to develop personal control over their lives. The words and phrases that he used were supplied by the Inner World, the Brotherhood. These words were chosen because of their specific energetic effect on the tribesmen Muhammad attempted to teach. Taken out of context and offered to another group, or spoken in daily prayer, these words are spiritually meaningless.

As people approach the first initiation they begin to learn, in a very rudimentary way, how their actions affect others outside of themselves. Muhammad was also trying to teach people about the effects of their behaviors. He directed people toward the idea of seeing other tribes as neighbors rather than enemies, and he tried to lay the groundwork for the people of the Arab World to unite.

This unity was proposed as a way of stopping war and violence, and helping people see that they must begin to respect one another if ever they were to find peace in their lives. Muhammad was not attempting to form a religion. His work was not meant for millions of souls. It was directed at only a few souls who could potentially prepare for the first initiation. None of the Muslims today are preparing for the first initiation through the Islam club. In reality, through Islam all practicing Muslims are moving further into darkness every day.

Muhammad had no energy directed at forming a religion club. His followers, however, sought religion. His early followers misinterpreted him and wanted to take political and emotional control over people's lives. Humans founded Islam. In fact, as human beings these people were some of the worst people on the planet. And that is what Islam energetically attracts to itself today—some of the worst people on the planet. Islam attracts violence, chaos, and confusion. It attracts greedy, power-hungry cutthroats who will seek power at any cost. Islam is the darkest of the world religions and the Islamic countries are energetically the blackest places on the planet earth.

MUHAMMAD

Muhammad incarnated as a second degree initiate. At the second initiation souls automatically enjoy a certain amount of power over the physical world because they are able to control normal human impulses and outbursts. Muhammad was preparing to take both the third and fourth initiations in a single lifetime. This was an extremely rare spiritual situation and one that would have normally been nearly impossible during Muhammad's time in history. However, Muhammad was a great soul and he died a fourth degree initiate, but not without an extremely difficult human life.

In order to accomplish the third initiation, a soul must be willing to open his or her heart. Opening the heart means that a person both sees and feels the suffering of other people. They see the pain in human relationships, and feel the hurt that people inflict on one another. When Muhammad opened his heart, he was forced to face a very black world. He was surrounded by murderers and thieves. Yet, he knew that he would have to attempt to provide spiritual leadership to these tribesmen.

Muhammad was very reluctant to fulfill his mission. He had many doubts about what he felt he was being told to do. Reluctance and doubt, however, are signs of a true spiritual leader. Genuine spiritual leaders must be in direct contact with the Brotherhood and must have at least indirect contact with a seventh degree initiate. Otherwise they are merely religious leaders, or some other kind of charlatan or fake. Spiritual leaders must have this rapport with the Brotherhood through telepathic communication. They must follow the information they are given, even though to do so usually means the person will be initially very unpopular.

Muhammad had such telepathic rapport, but he hesitated to act on what he was hearing until his inaction became too unbearable. Religious leaders have no such communication with the Brotherhood. They have only the echoes of their own minds. They have no doubts or hesitations because they do not care what their words might do to others. They care only about controlling other people and they have no hesitation about obtaining the power to do so. They do not question their own actions because they have only a single desired result—power over other people's lives.

If people were to look at Muhammad's life, they would see that he was not interested in accumulating wealth or fortune. In every respect, as he began to fulfill the requirements of the fourth initiation, he enjoyed less and less of the physical world luxuries. He was not attempting to gather power that would be used for his own personal gain. It is true that Muhammad had a certain amount of power. This power was much more spiritual, however, than it was political. He used this power as a disciplining parent must use power—to prevent a child from harming himself or herself. When parents are providing discipline or protection for their children, they are not trying to win votes or become popular with their children. They are just trying to do their job as parents.

Muhammad was just doing his job. He was not always very popular, but he was not trying to win votes. He was trying to teach an unruly group of tribesmen the most rudimentary forms of devotion, respect and unity. The religious leaders of Islam are trying to win votes. They are amassing wealth and fortune at the expense of their people, and they have nothing spiritual to offer whatsoever.

ISLAMIC RELIGIOUS LEADERS

The Islam club has no spiritual leaders. It has many religious leaders who use their roles to obtain political power in the Arab world and in other countries influenced by Islam. The religious leaders of Islam are some of the darkest people in all humanity. They have separated the Arab world into chaotic, violent factions causing the people of Islam to live in complete disruption and confusion.

The religious leaders of the Islam club represent the worst qualities of the followers of Islam. They are energetically much more disturbed and out of control than Muhammad's students. Although the leaders of Islam today live in a civilized society, they are far more barbaric and uncivilized than Muhammad's tribesmen. They have become even more corrupt since the discovery and harvesting of oil in the Islamic countries of the Middle East, because of the vast wealth and fortune that oil has brought them.

Islamic religious leaders believe they are the descendants of Muhammad. Yet in reality, there is no spiritual similarity between Muhammad and men like the Ayatollah Khomeini and others who have attempted to lead and unite the nations of Islam. As We have stated, Muhammad had a certain amount of political power which was granted to him by the necessity of his own mission. He used this power only to accomplish his work. Khomeini and other Islamic leaders have distorted the purpose of Muhammad's political power. They have interpreted this power through the hungry eyes of the human ego. They have decided that the obtaining of political power was part of Muhammad's message, and that Muhammad wanted all the nations of Islam united in religion.

Khomeini and others have spent their lives seeking power rather than the spiritual growth of humanity. Khomeini has sought to unite the Arab world, but not to teach people about unity. He has sought to gather enough power to overcome what he thinks of as Satan's superpowers—the United States and the Soviet Union.

Khomeini is a fanatical madman. He understands the primitive nature of most Muslims. He knows how to energetically incite people. He knows how to prey upon people's emotions and weaknesses. He put this knowledge to work in Iran when he took control from the Shah in 1979. He proclaimed his takeover as a religious act. He drew Iran's fanatics and madmen into the streets. He executed thousands who would not comply with his ways or who posed a potential threat to his position. The Ayatollah Khomeini, like other Muslim leaders, murders and destroys—in the name of Allah and the Islamic Revolution.

Khomeini is a religious leader, so he has no doubts about what he does. He did not hesitate to take control of the nation of Iran when he saw a possible opportunity to do so. He was and is unconcerned about his people.

The nations of Islam have no unity because the leaders of Islam are power-hungry, disturbed fanatics who use religion to control and even destroy people's lives. These leaders are usually very wealthy and have accumulated financial resources beyond what they could use in a hundred lifetimes, while many of their people remain impoverished. These leaders believe that if they pray several times a day according to Islamic law, they can then do anything they want in the name of Allah. This is the Muslim version of personal salvation.

When the Arab world began to produce oil, the greed and hunger for power increased. Religious leaders became more interested in political power and the Arab world became more chaotic and black. The oil industry brought out the greediest of men. These men met for several months in late 1985 and early 1986 trying to reach some agreement on limiting oil production in the Arab nations. The price of oil had dropped dramatically due to increased supply. However, their individual greed prevented them from reaching any such agreement. In spite of the fact that all these men were already wealthy beyond their capacity to spend, no one was willing to limit production because each was afraid of the money that might be lost.

Muhammad was serving humanity on behalf of the Brotherhood. His lifetime represents an example of service and a relatively small spiritual event. Khomeini and other leaders of the Muslim world have managed to take that event and distort it into one of the darkest religious and political travesties in the history of humanity.

RITUALS

The Islam Club, like the Jewish and Catholic clubs, is ridden with meaningless rituals. Like the Jewish club, these rituals treat male

Muslims as superior to females. Male children are expected to study and to learn the ways of Islam, while female children are expected to learn how to serve their husbands as slaves would serve a master. The rituals of Islam support the mistreatment and abuse of women, as do most religious rituals.

The religious laws of Islam are very rigid. They call for certain clothing to be worn and certain foods to be eaten. They call for extended periods of fasting and many prayers to be said at specific times during the day. A certain percentage of income is given to support the already wealthy religious leaders. Muslim children must study the Islamic tradition from a very early age, and people are expected to travel to Mecca to pay homage to Allah every year.

These rituals, like all religious rituals, have absolutely no spiritual meaning. They do not connect a person to his or her own soul or aid anyone in the process of evolution. The rituals of Islam do, however, consume people's lives. They prevent people from looking for something better or seeking something more real. Muslims spend many hours of every day in prayer. They dress, think, act, talk, and experience the world as Muslims, which is an extremely narrow and endarkened view. Of all the world religions, Islam has managed to tie up and misuse the most human resources. Islam has energetically engaged people in a way that causes them to focus their entire lives around their religion, with no energy left for anything else. Islam is the complete energetic focus in a Muslim's life. There is no other focus of attention. Part of this has come about because Islam is not only the religion, but also the nation. Church and state are one. The lives of Muslims are as narrow as human lives can possibly be.

The rituals of the Islam club keep Muslims completely oblivious to the realities of this planet. These rituals cause people to construct psychotic, dark little worlds and then to energetically manage their lives within these unreal systems. The more rigid and ritualistic a religion becomes, the more unbalanced the followers of that religion actually become, and the more that religion tends to attract similar followers. The followers of Islam are very disturbed. As a group, they represent the most disturbed people on the planet at this time. People need only look at the chaos and turbulance that occur in these countries each day. These countries are clustered together in darkness along with Israel, which is endarkened by Judaism—the second most disturbed religion in existence today.

The rituals of the Islam club are all human distortions of Muhammad's teachings. These rituals have no meaning in present time. They are basic, rudimentary notions that were once offered to people to help them begin to grow. When children are in kindergarten, they learn simple, basic math and language skills. Then they go on to the next twelve grades. The teachings of Muhammad were meant for souls who were in a kind of spiritual kindergarten, and only for this group of souls. Muslims keep themselves at the bottom of the evolutionary ladder by adhering to these rituals. It is as though they are potential twelfth graders who attended school every day for twelve years and learned only rudimentary math and language skills, learning nothing beyond those kindergarten skills. Muslims keep themselves in a kind of spiritual kindergarten by practicing these daily routines. Their souls have no opportunity to grow and go on to the next grade or step in evolution. Islam offers the perfect system of complete endarkenment.

MUSLIM WOMEN

Religion clubs in general tend to prevent women from taking on any leadership roles. Religion clubs usually look upon women as inferior to men and undeserving of full participation in services. This treatment—or more accurately mistreatment—of women speaks to the element of darkness that is involved in religion. The more a religion prevents women from participation, the more endarkened is that religion.

Islam treats women as slaves and servants because Islam is protecting the darkness. If the Muslim women (or women in any religious organization) were to gain power, that religion would begin to change. Religious leaders understand this. They want religions to stay the same, so they keep women from leadership roles. The reason that women leaders would change religion is that women are much less programmed into obtaining political power, wealth or prestige. Over a period of time women would naturally seek to turn religions into real service organizations, because women are generally much more interested in the well-being of humanity, and much less interested in personal gain.

Islam, as the darkest of all current religions, treats women in the worst possible way. Muslim women are not allowed any leadership or influence in the Islam club. They are given very little choice in determining what happens to them in their lives. Some Muslim women are called by a name that means mother of a son. For example, if her son's name was John, in Islam the woman would be called Mother of John. She would not be called by her own name. Muslim women are dressed like Catholic nuns and treated like prostitutes.

Male children are always preferred over female children. Muslim sons are taught to study the religion of Islam. Muslim daughters are taught to act like slaves to the men in their environment. Old Islamic laws prevented women from leaving their husbands, no matter how deplorably they were treated. These old laws are still in effect in some areas where women are badly abused in the name of religion. These laws were supposedly designed to protect the family as a sacred and holy unit. Abusing women is not sacred, nor is it holy.

Muslim women fulfill only those tasks that a servant or slave would fulfill. They have no access to learning any physical world realities. The religious leaders of Islam—like other religious leaders—understand that their religion would begin to change if women gained any skills connecting them to the real world. If Muslim women became connected back into reality, the Islam club would begin to change. However, the male Muslim leaders have designed a perfect system to prevent Muslim women from relating in any way to the physical world realities. Their women live encapsulated in robes and veils. They speak only when spoken to, and they have no place in the leadership of their religion or their country.

Muslim women are energetically attracted to the nations of Islam because they are very damaged souls. As a group, they carry past-life histories of physical and mental abuse. As souls, they view earth as the planet of despair. They have been magnetically drawn into suppressive, abusive cultures for so many lifetimes that they know of nothing else. They are like the souls in parts of India who keep getting drawn back into abject poverty and starvation. These souls have no hope of anything better. Often they are the ones who do not reach the higher planes of the Inner World between lifetimes, where they could be repaired and healed. They simply continue to incarnate with the same damage and hurt over and over again. In each consecutive lifetime, they amass more of the same pain and hopelessness.

Islam is constructed on human power games that are played at any cost in the name of religion. Islam willingly takes advantage of these damaged souls and keeps them powerless and despairing. Muslim religious leaders know these women will not fight back. These leaders know that Muslim women are bankrupt with no resources to break from their lives of slavery and their lifetimes of suppression. Muslim women carry a very low, heavy vibration caused by depression and despair, that continues to become more painful and hopeless in their lifetimes as women of Islam.

MUSLIM MEN

The Muslim men of today still think like the cutthroats and thieves of Muhammad's day. They believe that religion is to be used as a political power base. They study to become religious leaders, but they are really studying about political power. As a group, they are extremely dishonest people. They are cheaters, robbers, liars, and thieves. The men of the Islam club energetically represent some of the darkest characters in all of humanity.

Muslim men, like Jewish men, generally refuse to involve themselves in tasks that would keep them connected to physical reality. The more a Muslim man aspires to become a religious guide or a mullah, the less likely he is to be involved in any reality-oriented tasks. He is more likely to spend his time studying the ways of Islam than learning anything about human relationships.

The Islam club attracts souls who have spent lifetimes in corruption and chaos. Islam trains Muslim male children from an early age to learn the ways of Islam, which is really teaching them about corruption and political power. While the men say their prayers at seven o'clock in the morning, they think nothing of cheating their neighbors in the marketplace from eight until noon.

In reading the history of Islam, one can see that it is not a spiritual story of men attempting to respect one another and live in peace. It is a political story of a religion that is used for political gain. It is a story of war, fanaticism, and violence that continues every day in the nations of Islam. It is a story of the most perverted, distorted use of the male polarity. Muslim men do not relate to the women they marry, nor to the children they bear. They have no idea what a healthy marriage would be like, or how to even begin to respond to the emotional needs of another person. Their families are like slave camps and their relationships are as irresponsible and loveless as human contacts can possibly be.

Yet each day, in the name of Allah, Muslim men self-righteously worship in prayer, as though their rituals could exonerate them from any responsibility for their actions. Muslim men like their political power games, and find excitement from the violence and confusion that plague their countries. They place no value on human life and think nothing of watching war occur in their streets. They believe their turbans and robes give them license to do anything to keep themselves in power.

THE COMMUNISM CLUB

Although there are many religion clubs in Eastern Europe and the Eastern world, We would consider the Communism club the most prominent. Communism is not usually considered a religion because people do not yet understand the nature and source of religion clubs.

Religions have generally arisen out of dissatisfaction. They are formed because people are reacting against something they do not like. For instance, Martin Luther became dissatisfied with the Catholic church. He saw that the Catholic club had become a corrupt political force in the world. He knew that it was wrong for people to misuse power as the Catholic religious leaders misused power. He knew that many of the Catholic doctrines and dogmas were ridiculous, and that accepting the idea of an Immaculate Conception was insanity. Yet, he was not evolved enough himself to do anything except start an equally useless religion. Out of his dissatisfaction with Catholicism, he founded the Lutheran club.

Like the Catholic club, the Lutheran club offers nothing of value or meaning to its members. Lutherans are not being healed of their human suffering in any way by participating in the Lutheran church. They are not receiving spiritual direction of any kind, nor are they provided with even the most basic human comfort in times of crisis and loss. They are getting the same thing that the Catholics are getting—meaningless religious cliches. Like Catholics, Lutherans invest only in personal salvation. Therefore, they do not have to change anything about themselves because they have already been saved.

Communism was also founded out of dissatisfaction. Marx, Engels, and others could clearly see that the industrial revolution and the rise of a perverted system of capitalism were causing extreme exploitation of the common man. They knew that the perverted version of the capitalist economic system would support the rich at the expense of the poor. They knew that in such a system someone was bound to suffer. Obviously they were correct in their thinking.

However, none of the early founders of Communism were evolved enough to promote a correct, spiritually-based system. They could construct only another human system burdened with all of the same human extremes as capitalism. Marx and the early Communists saw capitalism as an extreme system with a great discrepancy between the treatment of the rich and the treatment of the poor. Yet, Communism is one of the most extreme economic and political systems in the world. Communism exploits people in ways that even the most perverted capitalists could not contrive. Communism functions exactly like a corporate system. In fact, Communism is the ultimate corporate structure. People who live in Communist-controlled countries can expect to be treated much worse than people who live in Western capitalist societies.

Communism has its own "Bible" written by Karl Marx, which is as useless to people as the Christian Bibles. Communists have their own "savior" which they call comradeship. Comradeship is nothing like genuine brotherhood. Communists look to comradeship for salvation in the same way that the Christians look to Jesus to be saved. Communism ties up people's resources and energies in the same way that religion clubs do. Communist governments offer people made-up fantasies about the governments of their countries, lying to them about the economic and political systems and frightening them into being controlled, just like religion clubs. Communism prevents spiritual growth by leading people away from the real problems in their lives that need to be solved. Instead, Communism directs people into a system of government that requires all their resources just to survive. Individual spiritual evolution requires a political and social system where each soul is free to find a natural, correct path. However, like other religions, Communism tries to herd people down a single, unnatural human way.

SUFISM

This book contains information that is relevant to healing the mental-emotional conditions that prevent spiritual growth in Western nations. The healing instruments and Soul Readings, offered by the Brotherhood through Gentle Wind Retreat, have been designed to solve the mental-emotional problems of people in Western societies. This series of books, and the healing instruments, would not match the ideas and expectations for relief in people of the Middle and Far East who have not been as influenced by Judeo-Christian tradition. Islamic nations, and other non-Western countries, must look to a form of relief that fits with the ideas and expectations for their societies. Such relief is available to these societies through Sufism.

Sufism is not a religion, although in its perversions it has been presented as one. Sufism is a road to evolution, if practiced without human distortions. The Brotherhood works through certain Sufi communities at this time to bring relief to the Eastern world. It should be understood that the Brotherhood is not working with Sufi groups in the Western world because this is not the most expedient road of evolution for Western societies. Further, the Brotherhood is not working with all Sufi communities in non-Western countries. Some Sufi groups are too overrun by human power and control to have room for the Brotherhood.

Sufism offers a symbolic understanding of the levels of initiation and the existence of a governing body called Hierarchy. Sufism understands the need for spiritual focus rather than human focus, and attempts to help people shift their focus out of the physical world toward the spiritual world. The Sufis teach people about their own individual divinity.

For Muslims, the Sufi teachings can help them break away from the idea that divinity exists only outside of themselves. The Sufis see the relationship between spiritual growth and the way a person lives. In this way they understand that one does not simply perform some Sufi ritual and gain eternal reward. Sufism acknowledges the need for spiritual responsibility. This concept is directly opposed to the ways of Islam where people can do whatever they want to one another in the name of Allah.

There are specific meditations taught in some Sufi communities that would benefit many souls now caught in the darkness of Islam. These meditations and Sufi exercises are nothing like the meditation techniques used today by Westerners. The Sufi techniques cause alterations in the consciousness that are necessary for evolution. These methods would be perverted by most Westerners who would not grasp the importance or meaning of the Sufis' message.

For the most part, the people of Islam have rejected the valuable aspects of Sufism. In some Islamic nations, Sufis are persecuted as religious heretics—which may indicate the resistance of Muslims to any real light or hope for spiritual growth.

Sufism offers the people of Islam a possible means for evolution to take place. The Brotherhood attempts to reach the souls of the Islam club just as We seek to reach souls in all parts of the world. Sufism provides the proper framework and technology to return some souls to an evolutionary path. Unfortunately, most of Islam is too endarkened to seek anything but more darkness, and too human-directed and power-hungry to look for anything genuine and spiritual.

6

FAITH

ALL RELIGIONS REQUIRE that people have "faith." Faith is necessary when people are trying to establish a belief in something that is not real. Religion clubs ask people to have "faith" in God, because what they are offering people are fantasy ideas about God. These fantasies have nothing to do with the real God or Logos of this planet. Because there is actually no such thing as personal salvation, religions require people to have "faith" that they will be saved. However, if people are willing to have "faith," they can then keep their lives exactly the way they want them to be. They do not have to change anything or look at anything about themselves that would cause them discomfort or challenge any of their pet ideas. They can simply have "faith" in the fantasy of personal salvation and do nothing to improve themselves, their relationships, or the world in which they are living.

People know their religion clubs are lying to them. They know they are being deceived, and that a weekly dosage of religious cliches or New Age enlightenment does not help them feel better or solve any of their personal problems. However, if they acknowledged that they were being lied to by their priests, ministers, and New Age gurus, their belief in personal salvation would be challenged. People simply will not allow such a challenge because they do not want to face the discomfort of actually having to do something about themselves. They would rather be drugged on religious cliches and promises of New Age "light and love" than to do any real growing. These "drugs," incidentally, are far less likely to be effective now that humanity has entered the Age of Aquarius. The Age of Pisces, ruled by Neptune, was a time of unconsciousness, sleepiness, and fog. Uranus, the ruler of Aquarius, is not so generous. People will no longer be allowed to go to sleep on themselves through the use of meaningless words.

Some would claim that they were healed at a religious service. They know they were healed because they felt some energy or electricity run through their bodies. In fact, a very small number of people on occasion are healed. The healing these few people speak of produces no spiritual results, but it may produce some mental-emotional relief. People have a normal flow of energy through their bodies. This energy is conducted by the human electrical system called the meridian system. When energy is blocked for some reason, the person has a breakdown in his or her electrical system that is experienced as a mental-emotional upset or physical imbalance.

When the right minister speaks about religious gibberish in a way that mesmerizes people, some of the people suspend their normal beliefs, thoughts, worries, and feelings long enough to listen to the minister, particularly if the preaching style is dramatic and loud. When this normal activity is suspended, the blockage in the meridian system can be released. The person will then experience a sense of relief and a sense of peace. The minister is usually saying something like, "Heal in the name of Jesus." He might just as well be saying, "Heal in the name of Ronald Reagan." Jesus has nothing to do with the relief. It is the suspension of normal mental-emotional activity that causes the release of energy and the feeling of relief. However, people are so convinced they have been saved through Jesus, that they use their experience of relief to confirm their religious fantasies. They deepen their faith. So even when they do experience this type of relief, they only use the event to become more invested in their irresponsible fantasies, and detach themselves further from the reality of spiritual evolution.

Ministers and priests promise people that their lives will change if they have faith in God. Yet, no one ever changes anything as a result of having faith. People only alter their course in life when what they are doing is causing them so much pain that they "change" simply to stop the suffering. Conversely, when ministers and priests talk about having faith, they are simply inviting people to adjust themselves into that particular church and their own brand of ministry. They are encouraging people to adjust to the songs that their respective churches might sing, the Sunday sermons, and the rituals of their particular clubs. When people have faith in this sense, nothing intrinsic in them changes at all. They are simply making the necessary adjustments into their religion clubs.

Occasionally, people talk about the fact that religion clubs and enlightenment clubs are lying to them. When they try to expose these lies, club members tell them they are having a crisis in faith. Their priests and ministers convince them that their crisis will pass and that they will see they were being tested by the devil. Therefore, if they pass the "test" they become even more entrenched in their religious ideas, because no one wants to be overtaken by the devil. In reality, investing in religious fantasies causes a person to be as overtaken as anyone can possibly be. The only real "devil" is the idea that people have been saved, and most of humanity has already been completely captured by this idea.

The Brotherhood is not asking that people have "faith" in this book. Rather, they ask people to consider what is being said here. It is not expected that people will relinquish their ideas of personal salvation. In fact, at this point that is not even possible. All that people can do is suspend their ideas of personal salvation long enough to temporarily question their investment in salvation or enlightenment.

Everyone, by virtue of their existence, is on a path in life. Most people are on a human path, governed by human ideas and goals. The human path is always contrary to the spiritual path. However, everyone must eventually complete the seven planetary initiations, no matter how long that may take. So, in a sense, you can either enroll in evolution now or in ten thousand years. Since the Logos of this planet is millions of years old, He has plenty of time.

The process of evolution is one of continuous movement and change. People who are evolving have climbed into a moving river.

They can see that there is a natural current to the river, and they have found a way to move forward with that flow. Each person in the river moves in a way that is unique to that individual. Some people are able to swim with the current and move very quickly. Others are floating on their backs or on rafts. Some people have climbed up on the backs of the swimmers, and others are rowing in small boats. There are even some who are in the river but are trying to swim against the current. Fortunately, they sometimes tire themselves out enough to be taken forward by the current while they are resting.

There are billions of souls on this planet. Very few are actually in the river. Many more are standing along the shore. Some are standing in the mud. Others are standing on the rafts and in their boats. They are all watching the movement of the river as it passes by them.

The ministers, priests, rabbis and New Age gurus are also standing along the shore. Each day, they tell the people along the edges to have "faith" that they, too, are in the river and moving. Some have been watching the river move for so long that they think they are moving. However, in reality, they are all sinking further into the mud.

Occasionally, someone like Jesus or Gandhi comes along in the river. The people see this person working his way down the river by moving with the current and flow. For a brief moment people see that they themselves are not moving. However, rather than facing the fact that they are standing still, they try to drown the person who is passing by in the river. Souls like Jesus and Gandhi are killed when they attempt to show people the reality of the moving river. The people who kill them then make up fantasies about what these souls were doing so they can continue to have "faith" in their fantasies—such as salvation—and never face the reality of the moving river.

FAITH IN RELIGIOUS LEADERS

When religious leaders ask people to have "faith" in what they are saying, they are really asking people to invest themselves in the religious leader's particular damage. Imagine a long assembly line of cars. At the beginning of the line, the cars are only rough frames. At the end of the line, the cars are painted, fully equipped, and ready to be driven away. All along the assembly line, the cars are being fit with the necessary parts to produce a perfect, finished product. At various station points, there are inspectors who must make sure that the cars are being assembled properly.

Spiritual evolution is like a long journey through an assembly line. Souls begin as rough frames. Over a series of lifetimes, if all goes well, they accumulate the necessary energies to produce a perfected vehicle. In order to come off the assembly line with a proper spiritual construction, souls must remain on track and complete the production line process. Otherwise they will not be perfect finished products when they come off the line.

Religious leaders could be thought of as self-appointed inspectors who know nothing about how a car is constructed. They have heard about what cars should look like when they are driven off the factory lot, but they know nothing about how to produce a perfect, finished car. These self-appointed inspectors locate themselves at places along the assembly line where they themselves received so much damage that they fell off the line. As the unfinished cars come by, the inspectors yell at them for not being finished products. They tell the cars that they are evil and worthless; that they are sinners who should feel guilty because they are not yet finished cars. If these inspectors yell at some cars long enough, the cars will be thrown off the line and will pile up at the inspector's particular point in the line.

Most of these inspectors have fallen off the line in the very early stages of assembly. Most of them only know about very rough frames without any internal working engines or other parts. As the cars continue to be pushed off the line at that spot, they pile up into what the inspectors call a congregation. The more the inspectors condemn them, the more the cars tend to remain off the assembly line.

None of the cars in the pile-up ever question whether the inspectors are qualified to inspect the cars. No one ever looks into the inspectors' personal lives and backgrounds to discover whether or not they actually know anything about cars. The people who are most affected by these inspectors are the same people who would put $5,000 down on a piece of land in Florida without seeing it first. They are the ones who go to the real estate agent who shows them pictures of what the land could be like in Florida. The people then invest all of their financial resources into the land only to discover that the land is nothing but salt marsh. Their resources are gone and they have no land.

When religious leaders ask people to have faith in what they are saying, they are asking people to buy land without ever seeing it. They are asking people to accept them as self-appointed inspectors on an assembly line, even though they do not have any information about how to build a car. Imagine what would drive off the lots of some auto manufacturers if none of the inspectors knew anything about cars. Religious leaders have created the same kind of chaos in the spiritual world. In order for souls to get through the early stages of the assembly line, they must be able to do so without the interruption of a self-appointed inspector trying to convince them that salvation can be achieved by getting off the assembly line and listening to the inspector. Very few souls are vigilant enough to be able to see that the inspectors are damaged, disturbed people. People have such a great desire to believe in the fantasy of personal salvation that they will buy anything these inspectors have to say. But the moment they begin to invest their resources into these fantasies, they are on the same path as the landowner who invested his or her money into Florida salt marshes without seeing the land before the purchase. They are without resources, listening to inspectors give reports about their own personal difficulties in the form of projected criticisms of others.

LOURDES: AN EXAMPLE OF FAITH

Most people in the Western world, regardless of their religious club membership, have heard about the "miracles" at Lourdes, France. According to the Catholics, Mary, the mother of Jesus, appeared at this site to a little girl named Bernadette. Bernadette claimed to see this apparition on several occasions. From that time on, the spring waters of Lourdes were said to contain special healing powers. As reported in a 1986 "60 Minutes" news special, millions of people have come to Lourdes in hope of receiving a healing from these waters. Sometimes as many as 40,000 people a day come in search of relief.

In reality, Bernadette was a seriously disturbed schizophrenic who was having psychotic episodes. Catholic Church officials knew that Bernadette was disturbed, but felt that the Church needed a morale boost at that time. They felt that Bernadette's "apparitions" would be a helpful inspiration to a waning Catholic population. These Church leaders did not expect the "mystery" of Lourdes to go beyond their influence. They had no idea that the Lourdes business could gain so much momentum. When they discovered that the whole fantasy was out of control, they set up their own criteria for the healings and took over management and control of the activities of Lourdes. Then the Catholic Church declared Bernadette—the schizophrenic—a saint. Today, Lourdes is an elaborate Catholic club extravaganza.

Of the millions of people who have ventured to Lourdes, the Catholic Church claims sixty-four official healings. If the waters of Lourdes actually have some healing powers, why have so few found relief? In fact, if only sixty-four of the millions who have come to Lourdes have found relief, what are people doing at Lourdes? Many more people who never go to Lourdes experience unexplainable relief from physical and mental-emotional conditions. The spontaneous remission rate for certain cancers alone is much higher than the "miracle" rate at Lourdes. Statistically, people would be better off never going to Lourdes for relief. The number of people who get unexplained relief without traveling to Lourdes is much higher than the number of people who go there looking for a miracle that never happens.

The idea of Lourdes with all its glittering lights and legendary stories is very appealing to people who want to be saved. They like the idea that they can go to France and be "saved." In fact, they like it so much they cannot see that they would be more likely to find a miracle in Pittsburgh than at Lourdes. However, the travesty of this Catholic club hoax does not stop here. It is much worse. It is worse because most people become more passive and more spiritually deadened as a result of their pilgrimage. When people go to Lourdes, they hope to be saved by some miracle. When the miracle does not occur, they must increase their "faith" (and therefore their passivity) in something that is not real. For example, during the aforementioned "60 Minutes" news special, a woman was interviewed who had come to Lourdes searching for mental-emotional relief. She said she had come to Lourdes because her husband had died, and that this loss had left her with a broken heart. When the interviewer asked her if she felt any better as a result of her visit, she said that she did not feel better, but that she had more "faith" than she had before coming to Lourdes. Several other people with physical problems responded in essentially the same way.

All of these people come looking for something that Lourdes cannot provide. When they cannot find that relief, they settle for "faith." The same thing happens every week in churches all over the world. Church club members cannot find relief. Instead of becoming active and challenging the garbage that is being fed to them by their religious leaders, they become more passive and increase their faith in their favorite idea of personal salvation.

When people visit Lourdes, they get a religious lightshow, an elaborate parade, a lot of meaningless words, overpriced religious trinkets, and renewed "faith." When people hold one of the healing instruments offered to humanity by the Brotherhood, they get immediate mental-emotional relief and increased inner calm. The instruments are offered at no charge. The trip to Lourdes costs thousands of dollars. Next year millions of people will visit Lourdes, while only a handful of people will catch on to the reality of evolution. Humanity's preferences are more than clear. What can the Brotherhood do in the face of this reality?

MYSTERIES

To be a member of any religion club, you must be willing to accept mysteries. This is easy for most people since both formal education and religion promote mysteries by preventing people from connecting with reality. When religion clubs say that people have been saved, no one asks, "Saved from what?" No one asks because the "what" is an acceptable mystery. When Catholics proclaim their belief in the dogma of the Immaculate Conception, they make the conception, the birth, and the life of Jesus a mystery.

Evolution, in a way, is a process of unraveling mysteries in order to discover reality. The more mysteries a person allows into his or her life, the less spiritual growth is taking place. If Jesus had actually come to save people (which he did not), he would not have gone around telling people about it. He would have done it as an act of love. People have to know something is wrong when religious leaders tell them they have been saved, but then refuse to reveal what they have been saved from. The only thing that people have been "saved from" is the reality of their own individual evolution and the real sacrifices that must be made to accomplish spiritual growth. People willingly accept the mysteries of religion because they are trained through formal education to become disconnected from reality. Take Alice Smith, Ph.D., practicing psychotherapist, as an example. Every day Alice drives to work in her car. She knows that when she wants the car to go forward, she must push her foot down on the accelerator. She knows that when she wants the car to stop, she must push her foot down on the brake pedal. However, she knows nothing about what causes that car to move forward. She knows nothing about the conversion of fuel into energy that creates motion. These are mysteries to Alice. She has no idea what actually causes her car to stop when she presses her foot on the brake pedal because she does not know what lies between her brake pedal and the wheels of her car. This is another mystery.

If Alice actually knew anything about what happens under the hood of her car, she would have an entirely different approach toward people. However, Alice is not required to know anything more about reality than her local minister or priest. She is only required to pass the necessary psychotherapy courses dedicated to manipulating and controlling people through their damages. Everything else about reality remains acceptable mysteries.

Each week thousands of ministers, priests, and rabbis stand before millions of people and talk in religious cliches and gibberish. Some of these religious leaders are so sick and so disturbed that their sermons are nothing more than the ravings of madmen. Others ramble on into meaninglessness and nonsense. Yet, no one questions what they are doing or what they are saying because people accept the "mysteries" and fantasies of religion without question. The more a person accepts mysteries, the more drugged and unconscious that person can become. As a result, the reality of life and its real problems never have to be faced and solved.

The "mystery" of Lourdes brings millions of aimless souls to

France every year in search of help they will never receive. The "mystery" of the bread and wine brings millions of Catholics to the altar every Sunday to lower themselves into mental violence while they claim to eat and drink the body and blood of Jesus. Any back ward psychotic who expressed a wish to eat and drink someone's flesh and blood would be locked in an isolation unit. However, religions can get away with anything they want to get away with as long as people accept the idea of "mysteries."

Evolution is about reality. There are indeed things about evolution that human beings cannot understand, by virtue of the fact that people reside within the limitations of the human consciousness. But these are not mysteries. Once the cycle of death and rebirth is broken and reincarnation is no longer necessary, people can go on to learn of these things. Religions are about fantasy. They attempt—as does the educational system—to keep reality a mystery so their control over people's lives can continue. People are more than willing to allow reality to remain a mystery, because they do not want their fantasies of salvation (salvation from what?) challenged.

If you were to ask ten different religious leaders to tell you about your soul, you would receive ten completely different answers. You would get ten different answers because none of these people know anything about souls. Each one would make up a story. People would accept these stories because souls are mysterious. No one is expected to know anything about souls and people want to keep it that way.

Clergy, as a group, tend to be very intolerant of uncertainty or of anything that might cause them to feel a loss of control. These ego structures become easily agitated and begin to break down when confronted with the unknown. Once they are able to label unknowns as "mysteries," they feel that they have claimed control over those unknowns. Anything that causes them uncertainty is therefore entered into the file they have labeled "mysteries." To these ego structures, mysteries become as knowable as a can of tomato soup or a roll of toilet paper, because once the unknown is labeled it automatically becomes a known. Because the ego structures of clergy members are so damaged and so fragile, they are unable to face the uncertainty that is inherent in evolution. The more evolved a person is, the more uncertain their life actually becomes. Clergy members, therefore, are unable to grow spiritually or to know anything about spiritual growth.

VIGILANCE

Humanity has lost all sense of vigilance. As a result, people like the televangelists, minister-politicians and other disturbed zealots can get away with saying anything they want to say, and no one questions their words or actions. Vigilance requires people to be responsible listeners, discriminate about what they will accept and believe. Millions of people listen to these evangelists every week, mesmerized by their meaningless ravings, without accepting any responsibility for what they are hearing.

Spiritual evolution cannot be accomplished without vigilance. Religions teach people to relinquish all vigilance and to substitute faith. Vigilance requires that people stay conscious, aware, and responsible for their lives. Faith allows people to become passive, unconscious, and to lead irresponsible lives. Vigilance is necessary so that a person can gain control over his or her life in a way that allows the soul to direct that life. Faith allows people to live without any spiritual control or direction, guided only by the objectives and goals of the human ego.

In order for a person to reset the course of his or her life, human goals and objectives must prove to be dissatisfying. Only when a person is convinced beyond any doubt that the human goals are not satisfying is spiritual growth even possible. Arriving at this conclusion usually takes people a long, long time. If, for example, a man or woman becomes a successful executive, the human ego is not satisfied. It only seeks further success. Drug addicts are similar in that they only seek more and better drugs. They use drugs to fill the emptiness in their lives in the same way that the successful executive uses power and money. The drugs temporarily alleviate the pain of the void just as power and money provide a temporary relief. As soon as the drugs wear off the addict is out looking again, each time needing more and stronger drugs to fill the void. Although the drugs are making him mentally and physically sick, he does not stop until he reaches some crisis point. In the same way, some business executives will not stop until they have a heart attack or lose their families through divorce.

Each time the goals of the human ego bring a person into crisis, that person has the opportunity to gain vigilance. Vigilance is an attitude of watchfulness or resoluteness against the uncontrolled pursuits of the human ego. Evolution requires vigilance because to grow spiritually people must be able to see that the human world is always temporary and never satisfying. For evolution to occur, people must be able to gain control over how they spend their energies and resources. Some people spend their resources almost entirely on their makeup and wardrobes. Some spend their resources on the building and improvement of their ideal homes, as if their homes would be permanently rewarding. Others spend their lives earning money, as if money could provide satisfaction and fulfillment.

When people come into the human world, life offers them a schedule. Each lifetime offers a different schedule with different events. Most in humanity are completely unaware that they are living within a schedule of events. Generally, people only become aware of the schedule when they collide with an event. An event in the schedule might be a childhood illness, a death in the family, a divorce, or a tree falling on the house. Colliding with an event produces calamity. Each impact point offers a person the opportunity to see that life offers a schedule, and that the events in this schedule are designed to teach him or her about the limitations and disappointments of the human world. Although most people are jolted when they collide with an event in the schedule, very few are able to remain vigilant after the event passes. Most people only develop a temporary caution that disappears with the passing of the crisis.

When a soul experiences many, many lifetimes and collides with hundreds or thousands of human events, that soul may begin to catch on to the schedule. Unfortunately, this rarely occurs without much human pain and suffering. Once a soul catches on to the schedule, that soul can start to amass the vigilance and resoluteness required for spiritual evolution to occur. The soul begins to see that investing one's resources in the human world proves to be painful and dissatisfying, and that one's peace of mind and mental-emotional well-being is a much better long term investment. The soul begins to understand that there is "a time to sow, a time to reap, a time to laugh, and a time to cry," and that all of this is a part of the schedule.

Being vigilant does not mean that someone can *avoid* an event in the schedule, because the schedule is the nature of human existence. However, vigilance will allow a person to *expect* an event in the schedule, which changes the intensity of the collision and the impact. People without vigilance are speeding down the highway of life. They are traveling so fast they have forgotten why they got on the road in the first place. They are unaware of the people around them or the possible dangers on the road ahead. When a person without vigilance collides with an event, it is like someone hitting a pothole on an interstate highway at ninety miles an hour. The person loses control of the car, lands in a ditch, and then has to recover. He must then use all of his resources to recover from the accident and to repair or replace his battered car.

People with vigilance already know that the highway of life is full of holes, ruts, and surprises. They know they cannot afford to have "faith" that the highway is free and clear, because they have collided with reality too many times. People with vigilance know it is necessary to travel with awareness and caution, and to remain conscious of the road ahead. They know that the moment they start believing they have life all figured out, they will be jolted by an event in the schedule. They understand that knowing about the schedule does not give them any control over the schedule whatsoever. However, when they do collide with an event they are more likely to be traveling at ten or fifteen miles per hour. They do not lose control of the car and suffer the mental-emotional shock of a severe accident. They do not need to deplete their energies and resources recovering from the event, so they are more able to use the schedule of life for growth and learning.

Until a soul has gained vigilance, spiritual growth is not possible. When religions teach people to have "faith" instead of vigilance, people become spiritual cripples who stand on the edge of the river going nowhere. They lose all spiritual control over their lives and forego all responsibility for their own existence.

SCIENCE vs. RELIGION

In recent decades, scientists have flooded humanity with information. Each year the information becomes more intricate, complex, and overwhelming. Each year science reveals some new view of the universe, or more complicated technological advancements. To maintain their elitist positions, scientists further complicate their "discoveries" by presenting them in scientific language. This method of presentation insures that the "nonscientists" will be excluded from understanding or questioning the scientific discoveries. As a result, the ordinary, "nonscientist" citizen feels that he or she knows less and less about what is going on in the world. Scientists ask that people simply have "faith" in their scientific conclusions.

What scientists do not understand is that people are naturally curious about life, and that people also naturally seek simplicity. Scientists have been successful at separating out all the nonscientists in the world. However, they have also been successful at alienating most of humanity by unnecessarily complicating people's lives. The nonscientists of the world—which is most of humanity—resent this alienation and these complexities, whether they are aware of it or not. People talk about the "good old days" when life was simpler. They talk about "getting back to basics." What they are really saying is that they do not want their lives filled with a labyrinth of scientific ideas because it makes life too difficult.

People are already beginning to react to all the scientific complexities. Many people are using religion as a forum for providing counterbalance to the intricate scientific view. These are the people who want to return to the Bible. In their own way, they are trying to return to a more simple way of life. Unfortunately, this cannot be accomplished by consulting a book full of meaningless gibberish. Nonetheless, the attempt is being made throughout Western society to return to religion—and more specifically, the Bible—as a way of reclaiming a more simple way of life.

People are trying to accomplish their revolution against scientists by attacking schools that do not provide a "Christian" view of the world. They are fighting court battles over books they believe are not "Christian" in their nature. They are waging political campaigns in the name of Christianity and claiming that God wants a "Christian" President. They are battling against one another. The Evangelists are fighting the Lutherans while the Mormons argue with the Baptists.

However, what these reactionaries cannot see is that they are fighting the elitism and complications of the scientific world with the worst possible distortions and perversions of reality. They are using religious fantasies to fight scientific fantasies. The more they attempt to use religious fantasies as weapons, the more bizarre their fantasies become. Ten years ago people in the United States would not have tolerated a mixture of politics and religion in the way these two are being mixed together today. People would have thought that those seeking election because they are "Christian" were fanatical reactionaries. Today millions of Americans support these bizarre fantasies about God's interest and involvement in politics. In reality, the Logos of this planet is very concerned and interested in national leadership, but not in any of the ways people might think. If people want to imagine that God is interested in politics, they should imagine how concerned God might be about religious fantasy worshipers trying to run the United States from their perverted, distorted religious ideas. They could imagine some potential presidential candidate asking them to simply have "faith" that what he is doing is directed by God, while his behaviors are obviously very pathological and disturbed. If people would do this they could then begin to imagine the kind of interest God— or more accurately, the Logos—has in politics.

As the forces of the scientists, with all their unnecessary complications, meet with the disturbed ideas of the new "Christians" who seek simplicity through the Bible, humanity will be faced with the formation of a new, more endarkened religion. People do not yet understand energy. If they did, they would not misuse their resources in the way that all people do now. They do not understand that all religions, political governments, and economic systems are generated out of the energy created when two opposing ideas or positions meet. For example, the United States as humanity knows it was formed by the joining of the Northern and Southern states. During the Civil War there was a great disparity between the ideas of the people of the North and the ideas of the people of the South. Their positions were directly opposite on many matters, including slavery. In fact, people felt so strongly about their opposing positions that they were willing to fight the Civil War. Thousands of lives were lost, and much human suffering was incurred. Yet, in the end, these two forces joined to become one of the strongest nations in the world. Before the Civil War, the United States had no real world power. However, once the energy of the two polarities—North and South—combined, the United States became a world power.

No one knew this would be the result of the Civil War. In the same way, no one in humanity can foresee the result of the current collision between science and religion. There are no guns being raised yet. However, the energy invested in each position is very strong and deep, much more so than people can see. When these forces collide, the resulting energy will be more than sufficient to form a new and more endarkened religion. People can expect to hear more insane claims about God's interest in politics, school books, and morality. They can expect scientists to generate more inaccurate, complex ideas about human life and the physical universe. Then they can expect these insane, religious fanatics (and there are millions of them in the United States alone) to join the power-hungry, elitist scientists in forming the worst, most endarkened religion humanity has ever known. And if that is not bad enough, no one will even be able to figure out where this bizarre, disturbed new religion began.

SCIENTISTS: THE NEW MINISTERS

We have already discussed the fact that science has severely impeded the process of spiritual evolution. Science treats the physical world as though spiritual evolution does not exist. For example, science can now replace the human heart with an artificial heart, as though the body was not supposed to die. Science can keep the physical body alive for years by supporting only minimal signs of human life, as though dying was something to dread. People are actually supposed to grow old, or just finish their lives and die. Human bodies are supposed to break down and wear out. Many times the soul of a person sees that it has done all it can do in a given lifetime and simply wishes to move on. Sitting around in a reconstructed physical body or living chained to a daily medical program rarely produces any spiritual growth. Science refuses to acknowledge the existence of the soul, and therefore values only that which is temporary.

Scientists have offered humanity the quintessential path of human destruction. They have gained a position of influence in the world that is equal to modern day clergy. They are seen as the experts and are treated as a kind of new religious royalty. They are treated as though they have been given divine knowledge of the universe. Humanity regards scientists as having some monopoly on what is truth and reality, and what is not.

In reality, scientists have brought humanity to the brink of nuclear war. They have helped humanity poison the oceans, the air, and the land through "scientific advancements." They have prolonged human life in horrible ways, as though there were something wrong with death. They have taken the physical world and turned it into something hopelessly complicated for the human mind.

Science speaks of the scientists and the nonscientists. The scientists are the "experts" who create and understand complicated scientific language systems that the "laity"—the nonscientists—are incapable of comprehending. Scientists want humanity to believe that the future depends on their new scientific data. Yet, from the scientists' new data people will draw more incorrect conclusions about life, and find new methods to cause more pollution and danger to the environment. From this new data, people will develop new weapons and systems that would potentially destroy the planet.

Scientists are treated as royal experts. However, they are actually the ones, like the ministers, who know very little about the real world. Most scientists have received advanced degrees and have become the so-called specialists of the world. A specialist is someone who has so narrowed his vision that people can no longer eat dinner with him because he is incapable of having a normal conversation. An expert is someone who uses his or her mind to cover up a lack of knowledge about life. Imagine what scientists do not know about life! Most scientists are such "specialized experts" that they are incapable of relating to another human being. They have completely lost sight of the fact that the real miracles in the world rarely occur in laboratories. The true miracles are performed every day by the "nonscientist" carpenters who can build houses and shopping centers; by the "nonscientist" plumbers and electricians; by the "nonscientist" welders who construct bridges.

Most scientists do not know how to renovate an attic, fix a broken toilet, or rewire rooms in their homes. They are too busy being specialized experts to know anything about real life. Children are taught to worship the scientists. They are taught to value the work of the chemists, physicists and biologists. They are also taught to look down on the "uneducated" carpenters, plumbers, electricians, and welders. These "nonscientists" are actually the real scientists because they are the ones who know something about how the physical world comes together. Children are not instructed to see the "science" that is involved in constructing a house to withstand a hurricane, or a bridge that can tolerate thousands of pounds without collapsing. Children do not recognize that "science" is involved when a musician determines through the act of listening whether a sound is correct or not.

The scientific method has nothing to do with reality. Therefore, the conclusions drawn from this method are incorrect. So while the religious fantasy worshipers have constructed one non-reality, the scientists have constructed another. The non-reality of science is a product of the human mind, an extremely limited vehicle that tends to perceive most situations backwards. For instance, scientists think they have proposed a theory of the universe that encompasses its enormity and complexity. In reality, the human mind is only capable of perceiving a very small, narrow view of the universe. The universe is older than the mind can contain. Planetary Hierarchy extends upward beyond human comprehension. The laws that govern this universe—as grand as it actually is—are very simple, and therefore out of reach of the scientific mind. Science is a mass of incorrect conclusions about people and their lives. Scientists are trying to cover up their own lack of information about life by making everyone else's lives overly complicated. What they do not yet see is that people resent being treated in a condescending way. Physicians, for example, are now being confronted by patients who do not want to be patronized. Women are refusing to accept gynecological care from doctors who treat them like naive young girls. Patients in some hospitals have demanded patients' rights. The backlash against modern science and all its complications has only just begun.

7

ENLIGHTENMENT vs. EVOLUTION

MOST NEW AGE enlightenment seekers truly believe they have found some spiritual path. They do not understand that enlightenment means exactly the same thing as salvation to the human ego structure. The enlightenment seekers relate to their psychics, gurus, swamis, and channellers in exactly the same way that Christians relate to Jesus. The enlightenment seekers use New Age glamour and cliches about "light and love" in the same way that religion club members use religious cliches to numb their discomforts and avoid solving their personal problems.

Enlightenment is a fantasy just like salvation. When people invest their energies in obtaining enlightenment, they tie up their resources in yet another kind of religious fantasy. They lose all vigilance, paying no attention to what they are doing to themselves to achieve their fantasy of enlightenment. They are drawn to clever gimmicks, tricks, excitement, and thrills. They are not drawn toward anything that has to do with real evolution, because they have too many incorrect personal preferences and ideas about evolution to be able to grow. Like the religion club members, they are interested in evolution as long as evolution does not interfere with their ideas about enlightenment.

Most current New Age systems fail to produce any spiritual growth whatsoever. Even those that do generally leave people too damaged to move past the first or second initiation without years of repair work, and lifetimes of unraveling misinformation about spiritual growth. There are thousands of New Age therapies and techniques that promise enlightenment. All but a handful of these approaches are products of the human world, created out of the human mind. Anything that is born out of the human world can lead only to darkness. Nothing born out of the human world leads to anything but the human way.

Because enlightenment, like salvation, is just another human fantasy, no one ever arrives there. People are always searching for it. Their energies and resources become invested in what their lives will be like when they become enlightened. They imagine what their relationships will be like when they become enlightened, and how they will operate in the world. Because they are preoccupied with their fantasy outcomes, they have no resources left to solve their real problems. Imagine someone who is driving around in a car that needs serious repair work. The tires need to be replaced, the engine needs tuning, the oil needs to be changed. The person driving the car is always imagining what it will be like to drive his car once it is fixed. In fact, he spends so much energy imagining what it will be like to drive a smooth-running car that he has no energy left to do the work necessary to get the car repaired.

Since enlightenment seekers have lost all vigilance, they do not see the spiritual price they are paying for investing in human fantasies. Vigilance is necessary to stop oneself from investing in an outcome rather than in the work necessary to achieve that outcome. Vigilant people are not seeking enlightenment. They are too busy accomplishing real growth to waste their resources searching. Indiscriminate, unstable, disturbed people seek enlightenment, because they want to avoid this discomfort that is inherent in all real growth.

In recent years, the salvation seekers have adopted many of the enlightenment seekers' techniques. For example, in the 1960s and 1970s, weekend self-improvement workshops and seminars became very popular, and, in fact, remain popular today. Some of these workshops are designed to improve individual self-confidence and personal awareness, while others are intended for couples seeking to improve their relationships. In the 1960s, these seminars were generally run by psychologists, psychotherapists, and others who claimed to be interested in human development. Many religious leaders denounced these seminars and the values and attitudes supported by these workshops. They denounced these ideas as secular humanism and anti-religion.

Now, many churches are running their own workshops for human development. The Catholics call their most popular workshops marriage encounters. The Protestants have their own variations of the same thing. Many of the most prominent, outspoken ministers who denounce secular humanism, as it is called, are offering the same values and ideas in their own special seminars and workshops. The reason for this incongruity in the behavior of religious leaders is that enlightenment and salvation are the same thing in the human consciousness. One cannot denounce enlightenment and promote salvation, as these religious leaders are now discovering.

These workshops and seminars also serve a secondary function of keeping people involved in the religion. Keeping people involved in religion and giving them something to do is very important because it allows time to pass. The passage of time allows people to feel better. That is to say, people's problems change and even disappear over time, no matter what they do. If religions can keep people occupied long enough, people will automatically experience relief. Rather than crediting that relief to the passage of time, they will credit their various religions and, thus, continue to operate in the illusion of salvation.

Evolution is an ongoing journey. Evolution is not something that someone "arrives at" like salvation or enlightenment. When some New Age workshop graduates claim that they "got it," they believe they have arrived at enlightenment. However, since enlightenment does not exist, they have actually arrived at just another well-constructed human fantasy. They are really saying, "I have stopped. I am so full of my own fantasy of enlightenment that I am not growing any more." Some New Age seminar graduates are sure that they "got it" in the same way that Born Again Christians are certain they have been saved. Only a few souls of these seminar graduates are able to look at their lives through their seminar experiences in a way that allows them to take the first initiation. The first initiation means that a person is able to bring the most basic, violent human urges under control. Some seminars allow a few people to see the mental, emotional, and physical violence in their relationships enough to bring this aspect of the consciousness under control. However, when seminar leaders convince people that they "got it," they are leaving people with a serious disturbance that We call self-righteous positivism. It is impossible for people with self-righteous positivism to grow spiritually. And, as many relatives of New Age seminar graduates will attest, it is sometimes even impossible for these people to have normal dinner table conversations. While a few souls may have gained minimal evolution, they have become too burdened to continue growing. It is anticipated that the damages incurred through the accumulation of self-righteous positivism will take lifetimes to unravel.

Some enlightenment seekers think that traveling to India will help them become enlightened in the same way the Muslims think they will achieve salvation through an annual trip to Mecca. Those who travel to India or anywhere else in search of a guru who will grant enlightenment are exactly like the religion club members who go to their priests and ministers searching for salvation.

When people are evolving, they do not go to India looking for enlightenment. They do whatever is necessary to fulfill their own individual spiritual requirements which—for a very small number of people—might include a trip to India or Cleveland or Rio de Janeiro. When people are evolving they cannot afford to waste their resources on fruitless journeys.

People who think they can find enlightenment in India are perfect examples of people blinded by their own fantasy. India is a starvation-ridden, decaying nation where old religions and ideas go to die. Anyone with common sense and discrimination can see that India needs great help and support to recover from centuries of darkness. It does not need New Age enlightenment seekers to pillage the remains of a ravaged nation. Enlightenment seekers have no discrimination, common sense or vigilance. They have only their New Age salvation fantasies.

If people actually did find a real guru in some part of the world who could grant some form of spiritual blessing, ninety-nine percent of those who received the blessing would go backward in evolution. They would experience the "blessing" as having found enlightenment or salvation and would become even more passive about evolution. Things would get much worse for these people, not better, because they would be certain that they had been saved.

PURIFICATION

In the spiritual world purification is possible. Spiritual evolution is a process of purification that eventually leads to perfection. Unfortunately, this process has nothing to do with religion or enlightenment, and it is nothing like what people would imagine. Since most religions are based upon the illusion of personal salvation, most religions have developed "purification" rituals that they claim will produce salvation. Religious rituals and ideas of purification are all made-up fantasies that have nothing to do with spiritual purification. In the same way that salvation seekers look for purification in rituals, enlightenment seekers have their own rituals of meditation, fasting, and endless other choices.

By its nature the human world is a world of darkness and imperfection. People cannot purify themselves in the human world, or through any idea or technique that is born out of the human world. The more people fantasize and pretend they are purifying themselves in the human world, the more contaminated and corrupt they become. For example, the Catholics think they are purified by going to confession and receiving absolution. This allows them to pretend that all their "sins" are forgiven and that their souls are pure once again. For Catholics, this means they are free to go out and do whatever they please, because they can always be "purified" through confession—and still have no understanding of karmic law.

The Jews believe they can be purified by separating their meat and dairy products, and by refusing to do certain things (like driving a car) on the Sabbath. These beliefs allow the Jews to feel free to live the way they want to, because every time they separate their meat from their dairy they have purged their souls. They can do anything to one another—abuse their children, destroy their marriages—all in the name of Judaism, as long as they adhere to the rituals that keep them "pure."

Many Christians advocate baptism as a purification ritual. Baptism allows Christians to pretend they have been saved and purified by being submerged in water or pouring it over their heads. Then the Christians pretend that their souls have been born at the moment of baptism. This fantasy completely destroys their ability to face the reality of reincarnation and evolution.

The New Age enlightenment seekers think they can be spiritually purified through such rituals as macrobiotic diets. Most people who think they can purify themselves through macrobiotic living, or other dietary purification plans, lead very distressed lives, laden with hurtful relationships and painful situations. They cover their hurt and suffering with vitamins and herbs, or any of the New Age food purification fantasies. Some people may find physical benefits from these programs while others will find malnutrition. No one grows spiritually by changing what they eat. People have the same chance of growing spiritually by eating a vegetarian diet as does a homeless alcoholic living on back alley garbage. In fact, the homeless alcoholic is more likely to understand the work of the Brotherhood than most New Age enlightenment seekers, because at least the alcoholic knows he is on the wrong track.

New Age enlightenment seekers think they can purify themselves through meditation and other mind exercises. They believe that purifying the mind produces spiritual growth in the same way that health food fanatics believe that purifying the physical body brings this result. Meditation and other mind exercises may actually help to quiet a person's mind. However, no form of meditation or mental exercise produces any spiritual growth in Western societies, no matter how "purified" or relaxed a person claims to feel.

Human ideas of purification have taken many forms. Some are simply foolish while others are extremely destructive, causing much human pain. As an example, We repeat the fact that by 55 A.D. the Christians had so badly distorted and perverted the teachings of Jesus that humanity emerged with the sign of the Cross as a symbol of salvation. We have also spoken about the fact that the Cross is a symbol of violence to the human ego. When a body is draped over that Cross with blood pouring from the hands and side, the impression of violence in the human consciousness grows even stronger. To the human ego this symbol means that salvation is accomplished through purification, and that purification is accomplished through violence.

People cannot begin to imagine the death and destruction that have occurred as a result of this human idea of purification. As We have discussed, the Nazi Revolution actually occurred in an attempt to establish purification through violence. When Hitler massacred millions of people, he was operating on a human idea of purification. The same idea impelled Pol Pot to slaughter people in Cambodia in the 1970s. In the same way, human ideas of purification cause white people to mistreat, kill, or control blacks. Humanity cannot imagine the numbers of people who have been tortured and murdered in the name of purification. People cannot imagine the pain that is inflicted every day by political leaders who persecute dissenters to keep their governments "pure," or the hurt that is inflicted by people each day on their own neighbors because they are trying to protect their human ideas of a "pure" neighborhood.

Purification can take place only in the spiritual world. In a sense, evolution is a process of purification. In the early stages of evolution—in the first few initiations—the soul is attempting to regain control over the human ego. This is necessary for the soul to accomplish higher levels of growth. When a soul reaches the fifth initiation, the real purification process begins. In fact, if people want to believe in spiritual salvation, they should know that it does occur, but not until a soul has reached the fifth step. Religions tie up so much human energy and resources that even ambitious souls cannot go beyond the second initiation while they are involved in a religion. While religions claim to offer salvation, they actually prevent real spiritual salvation from taking place in the same way that New Age techniques and therapies prevent evolution.

At the fifth initiation the soul body drops away and the Monad, or spirit, remains. The Monad is the source or original cause of the soul. The Monad might best be thought of as one's own personal God. At the fifth initiation, the soul returns to the fiery or spiritual world. A fifth degree initiate living in the physical world in a physical body would reside in the spiritual world as well, in the sense that fifth degree initiates understand the human world. They have no more illusions about what the human world can bring or offer to them. They live in spiritual reality with spiritual goals only.

The consciousness of a fifth degree initiate is a body of light called the maya virupa. The body of light is a symbol of spiritual purification. All fifth, sixth, and seventh degree initiates are concerned only with attaining higher states of perfection. There are very few initiates at these levels residing in the physical world. Most live in the nonphysical world because living in the darkness and suffering of the human world is simply too painful once such spiritual purification has been accomplished.

THE THRILL SEEKERS

Most New Age enlightenment seekers have also become thrill seekers. They want the excitement and glamour that can be found at New Age Fairs and Expositions. They are not looking for anything spiritual. What they want are circus acts like the latest performing psychic or the death-defying thrill of walking on hot coals. These are the ones who want to know who is who among gurus and psychics. They like the white Indian dress and the dramatics of their psychics and channellers coming in and out of trances. They like the weekend seminar approach to enlightenment and the "quick and dirty" path to "spiritual success."

The thrill seekers like the idea of being attached to an astral entity, of hearing voices and seeing colors and lights. They like the astral videos of performers who walk through foggy streets in dream-like settings with flashing lights and unusual noises. They like the astral television commercials that advertise a car by surrounding it with fog and glittering women with enticing body movements. They like the astral beer commercials that take viewers through the blinking and flashing lights of city streets at night to find a Michelob beer at a smoky, foggy bar.

The thrill seekers like to listen to famous people talk about their psychic experiences, spiritual quests, and astral traveling as though this trash had spiritual value. Many of these thrill seekers are further off course and more mentally and emotionally damaged now than when they began their quests. They look in all the wrong places and find all the wrong people because they want excitement, not a spiritual path. They have found New Age glamour and astral thrills and have mistaken this junk for real spiritual evolution. New Age enlightenment seekers are looking for a fantasy of enlightenment that does not exist. They pay no attention to where they are going in the process of the search.

The thrill seekers are trying to launch themselves onto a spiritual path, but they will be unable to do so through excitement and glamour. They are trying to launch themselves out into the ocean by dropping their boats in a mud flat tidal basin at low tide. They are positioning themselves in a way that will make spiritual growth much more difficult. Evolution is a process of becoming less of oneself and of having less attachment to the human world. The thrill seekers have much more of themselves and much more attachment to the glamour, power, and money in the human world. Ten years ago most of these people could be reached spiritually; now they are completely inaccessible.

There are millions of thrill seekers and New Age psychic entertainers who make money from humanity's preference for glamour and excitement. There are groups who believe that a messiah is coming to save them. They have been announcing the coming of the Maitreya since the 1970s, even though they have been told by the Brotherhood that such an event is not possible at this time. However, they are caught in the thrill of the Maitreya's coming, and mesmerized by the idea of being saved. Their lives would be boring without the excitement of a savior's coming.

None of these people can see that if a messiah could come, such an event would not make their lives better. The coming of any potent spiritual force into the human world makes people's lives worse because it confronts all their incorrect ideas about spiritual growth. It forces people to look at how their human egos mismanage their spiritual resources. Those people who think that a Maitreya is coming to save them would not like the results if such a force actually came. They are so preoccupied with the idea of being the first ones to find this savior that they have all stopped growing. These people are more passive now than they were before joining their local messiah announcement club. They are as spiritually dead as the Christians who put their faith in Jesus and the

Muslims who put their faith in Allah. And they are so caught in the New Age thrill of a messiah that they are beyond real spiritual help.

ALICE BAILEY

The works of Alice Bailey were given to humanity as an experiment to see what humanity would do. The Brotherhood understood that the part of the person that was reading the information would not be able to grow spiritually as a result of this reading. It was hoped that people would see that the part of themselves doing the reading could do nothing with the information. It was hoped that people would become angry and frustrated enough to search for another part of themselves.

However, this occurred in only a handful of people. Only a few were actually inspired to grow. The rest of the people who read the Alice Bailey works became more spiritually passive. They fell into the normal human ego conclusion that they had figured something out about life. This is absurd since Alice Bailey did not understand her own writings. Those who went on to find esoteric schools to study the Bailey works, and others who followed an assortment of side paths, are in much worse shape spiritually than they were before launching into their mental fantasy worlds. These people cannot see that humanity is so burdened by the idea of personal salvation that people have forgotten the need to do more than read, pray, or meditate to accomplish evolution.

Like the Born Again Christians, the "Alice Baileyites" have arrived at righteousness. They are sure they have found the answers. Like the Scientologists, they are secure in their certainty. The Brotherhood calls the "Alice Baileyites," and other followers of esoteric schools, mental masturbators. They are like precocious three-year-old children who are able to read an advanced physics book. They are very proud of their accomplishments and can even recite some of the laws of physics. They can recite Newton's views and Einstein's theory of relativity. However, they are still developmentally at a three-year-old level, and they have never been in a laboratory. They have never taken measurements or done anything in real life directly related to the principles they are able to read.

Like the Bible readers and religious fantasy worshipers, the followers of Alice Bailey have it all figured out. Like precocious three-year-olds, they drop all the right words in all the right places in front of all the right people. Unfortunately, the spiritual effect for these esoteric students has been to become more passive about the actual hard work of evolution, and less spiritually accessible. They think they already know all the answers. Most people who involve themselves with the Alice Bailey club tie up all their resources with the mental ideas about evolution so that they have no energy left for real spiritual growth.

A very few souls have been able to use the information from the Alice Bailey books for growth. These souls comprise less than one percent of the members of the Alice Bailey club. Even for these ambitious ones, the road they have chosen is laden with difficulties. These schools cannot move a soul past the second initiation. People become too "certain" of themselves as a result of their esoteric study. They cannot relinquish the certainty of their own ideas, nor can they surrender to the uncertainty of real evolution. The "certainty" carried by these souls makes it very difficult for the Brotherhood to work with any of them.

The Alice Baileyites, and many others who follow New Age ideas of enlightenment, focus on the seven rays. Information about rays does not help a person evolve, even when that information is accurate. And for the most part it is inaccurate. Ray information would only be useful to people who had absolutely perfect etheric vision, and also the ability to transmit the correct healing to damaged areas in the etheric field. Perfect etheric vision would mean that a person could look at someone and see the breaks in the etheric web—the damaged areas—such as the gray and black crawling things that hang around cigarette smokers. More importantly, the person with such vision would have to have already evolved himself or herself up to a place from which the necessary healing energies could be transmitted. As of now, no one in the Alice Bailey schools meets either criteria.

People who are interested in rays are not interested in solving their own life problems. Almost everyone knows what their real problems are. People who want to use their time and their resources studying about rays do not want to look at themselves. They use their esoteric studies to prevent themselves from seeing their real problems. Those people currently studying about rays should look at their lives, and the lives of other students around them, and ask themselves whether their studies are solving their real problems.

The Alice Baileyites are the ones who tend to criticize this new series of books, and other current work of the Brotherhood, as being too negative. In fact, most of the New Age enlightenment seekers will find these new books very distasteful. These are the people looking for light and love. In the human consciousness light and love, wisdom and knowledge—all translate into humanity's favorite idea: personal salvation. These people do not want to read anything "negative" because they do not want their light and love, or more accurately their salvation fantasies, threatened or challenged in any way. As long as spiritual growth remains a mental process, the Alice Baileyites need to do nothing to grow. Like the Catholics and the Jews, they can continue to live in hurtful relationships, inflict damages on their children, become New Age "teachers" themselves, or do anything else they wish with their lives, because they have already been saved. They do not need to sacrifice their mental-emotional pain or any of their pet ideas about evolution, because they have found the Alice Bailey works and have been saved.

Others have also been given a role in the evolutionary plan. Jane Roberts has handled herself better than the rest. She allowed herself to be used as a channel without establishing herself as a guru to be followed. She maintained her identity as a writer and channeller of information, rather than claiming to be a spiritual leader herself.

Most people who claim to be channelling information today are either listening to the echoes of their own minds or they have connected with astral entities rather than the Brotherhood. In some cases their psychic information may be accurate. It is very rarely useful. Simply because someone is capable of being used as a channel does not mean that the person is capable of directing anyone in a spiritual way. J.Z. Knight is capable of channelling Ramtha's messages. However, these messages are as empty as religious sermons and are of no spiritual value. Mental ramblings about God or light and love do not produce spiritual evolution. They do produce spiritual passivity by causing people to think they can accomplish spiritual growth by paying someone for a psychic reading. People find anything appealing that lets them believe they can be saved without doing anything.

THE WORLD OF "MORE"

The human world is a world of "more." When people are fulfilling human goals they are always seeking "more" of something. For example, to earn more money some human egos invest their talents and resources in earning higher salaries. Their focus and resources are directed at the next pay raise. They have no regard for what they might be doing to themselves physically, mentally, or emotionally by focusing on "more" money. In these cases all the human ego wants is increased salary.

Some human egos want glamour. They focus their energies on their wardrobe, jewelry, hair style, car, and anything that will promote a glamourous appearance. Each year the fashion industry capitalizes on human egos that seek glamour by changing the styles and offering new and "more" glamourous clothing, jewelry, and makeup. Like the need for drugs or any human goal, glamour is a cover-up for emptiness and purposelessness. And, as with any human goal, there is never enough to satisfy the human ego.

Exercise, which never produces any spiritual growth, regardless of what people may think, is another example of the human need for more. In recent decades people in Western societies have discovered that exercise is in some way related to improved health. It is true that limited exercise does have some positive physical—not spiritual—effects. However, the human idea of exercise is that "more is better." As a result, millions of people in Western countries are literally running their physical systems into the ground. Running a mile or so every few days would produce great physical improvements in some people. Running five to ten miles a day is destroying internal organs as well as bones, muscles, and connective tissue in almost all who run these distances. Most of these people are literally running away from serious personal problems that need to be faced and solved. "More" exercise has simply become another cover-up for emptiness and purposelessness, and functions for people in the same way as "more" religion. When any energy or focus is directed at human goals, someone will always be seeking "more" of something. When human goals are involved, spiritual goals are not present. When religious leaders seek "more" followers, "more" money, "more" television and radio time, no spiritual goals are involved. Whenever there is a human personality who is gaining anything in the human realm, no spiritual leadership is involved. When the priests, ministers and rabbis gain "more" power and control over people's lives, no spiritual goals are present. When gurus amass cars, homes, and servants, they are not leading people on a spiritual path. They are offering a human personality, with human goals, that accumulates power and money at the expense of others.

When any one of the so-called New Age healers gains power, money, or fame for some technique that promises enlightenment, he or she is operating completely out of the human world. When these New Age leaders promise spiritual growth through seminars, books, meditations, crystals, tarot cards, psychic readings, or any other human idea, they are only perpetuating human goals. They offer human personalities to follow just as some televangelist ministers do. They want to make money, become well-known, and be interviewed on television and radio talk shows. They want to be invited to New Age carnivals where they can peddle their ideas to people who are interested in carnival thrills rather than spiritual growth. They want to become "more" of themselves.

Psychotherapy offers human egos a chance to become "more." Psychotherapists go to school to learn how to control and manipulate people through their own damages. The less a person knows about people, the more that person will seek credentials. Psychiatrists know less about people than any single group in all of humanity. To cover up this lack of knowledge, they seek "more" education and "more" degrees. People who specifically seek help from psychiatrists do so because they think that psychiatrists are "more" important. Although psychiatrists know nothing about people, people (human egos) think they will get "more" relief by seeing someone who is "more" important. If these same people received an invitation to come to the White House to discuss their personal problems, they would experience even greater relief talking with the President (even if they did not like him) than being with their psychiatrists, because the President is "more" important than their psychiatrists. They would feel more important themselves although neither the session with the psychiatrist nor the talk with the President would produce spiritual growth.

Any and all activity that produces more human personality or involves the achievement of more of anything in the human world cannot, by its nature, produce spiritual growth. Any religion, movement, therapy, technique, seminar, or book that involves a human personality cannot, by its nature, lead to spiritual growth. Any guru, yogi, or teacher of any kind who offers a human personality to follow cannot lead anyone to spiritual growth. Any religions, movements, therapies, or teachers who charge fees cannot provide spiritual growth, no matter how psychic, holy, visionary, kind, or enlightened they may appear to be. However, since humanity is at this time consumed by human goals, and all of their accompanying dissatisfaction, the reality of spiritual growth will be appalling and all the above information will be immediately dismissed.

THE WORLD OF LESS

The spiritual world is a world of "less." It is not a world of "less" alcohol as the Bahais or Free Willing Baptists would have one believe. It is not a world of "less" or no sex as the Catholics would have one think. It is not a world of "less" food or fasting as the Jews and others want to pretend. It is a world of "less" human personality—less deception, less manipulation, less suffering, less conniving, less withholding, less controlling, less hurtfulness, less competition, less jealousy, less presumption, less greed, less abuse, less false pride, less bitterness, less contempt, less confusion, less anxiety, less worry, less adventure, less thrills, less fright, less destruction, less excitement, less depression, less elation, less of everything that originates in the human world.

When a person asks, "What would I gain from the work of the Brotherhood?," the Brotherhood would say, "Nothing and even less." When people ask, "What's in it for me to grow spiritually?," the Brotherhood would say, "Nothing and less than that." People who are looking for something should continue to follow their religion, guru, swami, or psychic healer. They should not attempt to seek the work of the Brotherhood. They will only make themselves unnecessarily upset. People who are trying to get something out of this book should close it and throw it away. At this point in the book, the only thing people with these expectations have "gotten" is angry, because this information is meant for people who are seeking less—not more.

The path of spiritual growth cannot be traveled with trunks and suitcases filled with human "needs," desires, and goals. It is more like a journey that is taken with the clothes on your back and a toothbrush. By the time you get to where you are going, you lose even the clothes and the toothbrush. It is not a journey that the human ego takes with any pleasure. The soul finds satisfaction, but the human ego goes kicking and screaming. Most people who claim to be seeking spiritual growth are lined up in the train station with all their suitcases filled with human personality and human goals. They have trunks filled with resentment, contempt, deception, hurt, confusion, and they insist on taking them along. They have suitcases filled with human ideas about relationships, success, glamour, money, and personal growth which will not fit on the train. When the conductor comes to tell them that they must leave their trunks and suitcases behind, they get angry and hurt. They feel that they are being abused, punished, or insulted—all normal reactions of the human realm. They get so defensive and so intent on keeping their suitcases and trunks that almost all of them miss the train and must wait for another opportunity for real spiritual growth to come around.

The spiritual world, unlike the human world, is a world of satisfaction and peace. It is a world where fat people and skinny people are all the same. It is a world of real beauty that does not need to be covered up with makeup and glamour. The spiritual world is based upon honesty and reality. Therefore, people do not need to do unnatural, stressful things to cover their problems and hide their feelings. It is a world of fulfillment. Therefore, people do not need to work at jobs they hate or use drugs that destroy them to cover their emptiness, aimlessness, and failure. It is a world of genuine support beyond any human understanding. In the spiritual world people do not need to endure hurtful marriages or people

Voodoo

GR103. H8   1978
GR103.P8   19666b

Cult

BP603.S8 1977
BF1566.M8 1977

who hate them just to protect themselves from facing the mistakes they have made or to prevent themselves from having to live alone.

The spiritual world is as old as time. Much of what has been written in this book about spiritual growth could have been written millions of years ago, and it would have been true then in the way that it will still be true millions of years from now. Real truth is always timeless. People look to the Bible to find truth; all they find is gibberish. Rather than face the fact that they have found nonsense, they make up more gibberish and nonsense to help explain and interpret what they have found.

If people must have a "Bible," they would benefit themselves more by looking to the Tao (pronounced Dow). The *Tao Te Ching* was written in approximately the sixth century B.C. There are no Western translations of this work that adequately convey its intent. However, what is available would be more helpful to people than anything written in the Bible. Reading anything clogs the mind, but the *Tao Te Ching* could be thought of as a higher quality clog. When a person reads the Tao, his or her human ego becomes more neutralized instead of satisfied, which is always necessary if spiritual growth is to occur.

People will get nothing from reading the *Tao Te Ching*. They will get less than nothing and will discover how little they actually know. Unfortunately, when people in Western societies discover how little they know about life and people, they usually go to graduate school to learn "more." Graduate school then causes them to narrow their vision so severely that they see even less than before they received their degrees. However, they have their lack of knowing covered with an M.A., M.B.A., or M.Ed.

To the human ego system, the spiritual world is a world of fools. Yet, those who would be most condemning of this new series of books from Gentle Wind are the ones who believe that Jesus was conceived through an immaculate conception; that he died for our sins; that separating meat and dairy is holy; and that eternal reward is granted to anyone who reads the Bible. So, who are the fools?

This book cannot be understood by the human mind. If you, as the reader, feel that you now understand something, then you are in exactly the same difficulty as the Catholics, Jews, Muslims, Alice Baileyites, New Age seminar graduates, and anyone else who feels comforted by their understanding of something. People cannot grow by reading a book. If people could grow from reading, humanity would be evolved. However, they are not. People only think that they grow by reading which is why people read so much trash.

People cannot grow through words, at least the words that are being spoken and written today. People cannot grow through the ranting, raving, or writings of their religious leaders and enlightenment teachers because they are not the correct words. People need the right words, the right books, and the right information. Very little is available at this time.

However, even if people did have access to the right information, they would reject it. It would not be exciting enough or dramatic enough for people's tastes. Real spiritual leaders are not very interesting. People do not follow the real spiritual leaders because these leaders are too simple and too boring. It is true that he who says, does not know; and he who knows, does not say.

Some people will consider this book important, and it actually might be important to some souls. However, those who read it and use it to feel superior will only take this information and use it to support their own ideas of self-importance. They will not gain from it in any way. The Alice Baileyites are certain they have come upon important books, which is why they are spiritually lost.

The only thing that produces spiritual evolution is for a person to do exactly the right thing at exactly the right time. This is nothing that you could figure out with your mind or read about in a book. This occurs only when a person is directed by his or her soul. People who think they are listening to their souls are hearing only the echoes of their own minds. People who are directed by their souls have no thoughts about it; they are too busy following the directives of their souls to bother thinking about spiritual growth.

Religions have interfered with the voices of people's souls and have filled people's minds so that they can no longer grow. People in Western societies claim to be concerned about the current use of drugs like cocaine and marijuana. They are worried that these drugs will harm their children and cause them to use drugs as a way of avoiding reality. It is true that using drugs is a way of wasting one's life, and there are serious dangers inherent in any form of drug usage. However, these dangers are nothing like the spiritual devastation that occurs as a result of religions. All those people who are apprehensive about America's drug problem ought to be much more concerned about the world's religion problem. All those parents who are worried about their children taking drugs to avoid reality ought to be even more distressed about how their religions have taken people completely away from reality. They should be considerably more disturbed about the spiritual damage that occurs when a person is controlled and enslaved through guilt and fear. They should be much more worried about the damage that is done when a child is taught to believe that he or she can be saved through religion. These parents should have great concern about the purposelessness that their children feel. The children have no idea why they are here. In fact, if the children knew why they were alive, they would be far less likely to die from drug overdoses. The children would be far less likely to suffer from boredom and personal failure if their parents knew anything about evolution.

When the drug user inhales, injects, or swallows his drugs, he *knows* he is stepping out of reality into a drug-induced state. He knows that he does not want to be in reality, usually because reality offered him too much personal failure. When the religion user swallows the idea that he has been saved, he does *not* know that he has stepped out of reality. He does not know that he has eliminated all possibility of spiritual growth and trapped himself in a deadly fantasy. When the heroin addicts or cocaine users allow the drugs to dominate their lives, they usually become very sick and desperate. Many die from physical problems. They usually reach a point where they either die or stop taking drugs. However, the religious fantasy worshipers have no idea how sick they are; they keep taking religious "drugs" for hundreds or even thousands of years. They are spiritually sick and desperate, but they do not know how sick or desperate because they are too separated from reality to know.

People in America and in most Western societies cry out for strong legislation against drug pushers and suppliers. They can see that the drug dealers are cheaters, liars, and manipulators who take advantage of people's hurts and damages. However, they refuse to look at the religion pushers and suppliers—the priests, ministers, and rabbis who prey upon people's hurts and damages. Humanity can see that the drug pushers control people through drugs, taking money to keep people in psychological bondage. Yet, these same people refuse to see that the religion pushers control people through guilt and fear, taking away people's power to keep them in spiritual bondage.

People do not want to hear that spiritual slavery is wrong, just as they did not want to hear that human slavery was wrong. They do not want to alter their comfortable, convenient lives or change their ways, any more than the slave owners of the 1800s wanted to change their lives. It is not up to the Brotherhood to determine what people do. Each reader must determine for himself or herself the accuracy of this work. Each must decide whether they want to keep their comfortable, convenient lives, or free the souls enslaved by religion. Unfortunately, most people will add this book to their mental trash collections or literally throw it away in disgust. They will forget they have even read these things and will return to the comfort and convenience of "knowing" they have already been redeemed.

8

WHAT NOW?

IN OCTOBER OF 1986, the Logos of this planet began a worldwide healing project. This project is an aspect of the larger Plan to restore this planet so that souls can resume their intended evolutionary path. Through the office of the Logos, healings have been sent to men and women of social and political influence throughout the world. These healings eliminate past life and present life damages in the human consciousness, and reconnect the human aspect of the person to his or her own spiritual aspect or Monad. Once this connection is established, the person is automatically returned to a more natural state of existence based on simple cause and effect. This means that these healings allow people to draw toward themselves the life situations necessary to promote their own spiritual growth.

Spiritual growth can only be accomplished through the failure of the human ego. This human aspect of a person must learn that its goals and objectives are chronically dissatisfying, and often destructive. As this is discovered, the person is more willing to follow the goals and objectives of his or her own spiritual aspect.

For the human aspect to experience the failure of itself, it must be able to see itself as it is, and then make the necessary corrections.

A very limited number of those people who have received the transmitted healings were already following the goals and directives of their own spiritual aspect or Monad. After the healings, their lives have become more satisfying and more peaceful. Most people who have received these healings, however, had previously been directed only by their own human goals and desires, which were established out of damage or the need to control other people. As these people have received the healings, they have started attracting the necessary life situations that allow them to see the futility of living for the human world only.

The political leaders of the world were the first group to receive these transmitted healings. Most of these men and women had gained political power because of their charisma and authority, rather than through their personal character or genuine leadership ability. They gained influence in the world because they could fool people, and because they wanted power. Modern education prepares the way for people to be fooled by their leaders. Children are prevented from learning anything about character because they are forced to sit in their classrooms and submit to the authority of their teachers, no matter what kind of people these teachers might be. As a result, "educated" people have no ability to discriminate a good leader from someone who only knows how to look good.

If you have been listening to the news since October 1986, you already know that what We have said so far is true. You know, for example, of many American political leaders who have been exposed with their "hands in the cookie jar." You can already see that once spiritual cause and effect are re-established, people cannot hide behind their political smiles while continuing to lead corrupt, dishonest lives. The spiritual aspect of a person will not allow this to happen.

The religious leaders of the world—particularly including the televangelists—were the second group of people to receive these healings. The restoration of cause and effect is allowing these religious leaders to directly experience the effects of their own ideas and actions. As a result of the long era of darkness, humanity has been too disconnected from themselves to learn from cause and effect, even from their most destructive personal behaviors. Most people have simply carried their destructive ideas and patterns from one lifetime to the next without being able to change. Restoring cause and effect allows people to break their destructive patterns because they are able to experience themselves as they are, and then make the necessary corrections.

Ironically, these healings have given most religious leaders their first real spiritual connection. This is especially true for the tele-vangelists. However, because they were so far off the spiritual track, the road back to reality will be long and difficult for some. Again, you would only need to have listened to the news since October 1986 to know that what has been said thus far is true. You have already observed the results of these healings in some religious leaders' lives, and you will see more effects in days to come.

The third group to receive these healings were movie stars and professional athletes. Thanks to the emptiness and meaningless-ness of modern education, many people invest in glamour rather than in spiritual growth. Most movie stars and professional ath-letes lead very empty lives. These healings are restoring cause and effect in these people in a way that motivates them to seek real relationships, and to bring their unrestrained human urges for ex-citement under control.

It might be slightly more difficult for you to verify this last statement. However, if you have been following the lives and ca-reers of certain professional athletes since 1986, you have probably discovered that these men and women seem to have gained control over what were once almost animal aggressions on the basketball court, football field and other arenas. You may have also noticed certain celebrities finding much more satisfaction in their family lives rather than in their glamourous personal careers. However, it will be up to you to further research and verify what has been stated in this section and throughout this entire book.

SO WHY THEM AND NOT ME?

Some people have asked us, "Why have those in power or influence received these healings and not the rest of the planet?" Our answer is that the Plan to restore this planet includes everyone. However, the restoration must have a beginning place. Healing people who have a certain influence in the world is a natural place to start, because those on the top always influence those on the bottom or those in the middle.

Healing world leaders is only a beginning. In recent months the Logos has begun another aspect of the restoration process, which involves transmitting healings to each of the nations on earth. These healings are being transmitted through the office of the Logos so that each nation can reclaim its own inherent natural resources, and souls drawn to a particular country will be able to learn the lessons that only that nation can teach. For example, the United States is a place where souls come to learn about honesty and freedom. Yet it is a nation laden with dishonest leadership. And the people there are actually only free to travel and to vote. They are not free to choose whether or not their children should attend school, nor are they free to stop supporting government projects they do not agree with or find undesirable. They are not free to say and do many things, but they do have a Bill of Rights, inspired by the Brotherhood, to help them maintain some of their basic freedoms.

In Russia, people are actually trying to learn about true brotherhood. One of their favorite words is "comrade." Yet their very language is so badly constructed that it breeds corruption and alienation, the antithesis of comradeship and brotherhood. Even if these people wanted to change, the Age of Darkness has left them without any resources to undertake the task. The Stalin era was the height of darkness for the Soviet Union; and still today many scars from that era remain on this nation which could only be repaired with resources which are far beyond the human capacities of the Soviet people.

Each of this world's nations has a part in the Plan. And none of these nations can fulfill its role without both the leadership based on the best interests of the people, and the resources to lift itself out of darkness. Thus, these healings have been directed to provide the leadership and the resources necessary to accomplish the restoration process.

The religious leaders of the world are also "on the top" in that they influence the direction and course of people's lives. They have, however, been leading people deeper into darkness and further away from real spiritual evolution, which is why it was necessary to write this book.

To resume a path of spiritual evolution, people must first be able to see that they have been misled. Healing religious leaders has allowed these leaders to expose their own dishonest lives, and their own lack of real spiritual concern. It has allowed many people to see that they are being misled, and to question who they are following and where they are being taken.

Healing movie stars and professional athletes is necessary because many people use these celebrities as role models for their own lives. As a result, people have become fascinated with personal excitement and glamour, regardless of the fact that neither ever leads to satisfaction or peace.

NO ONE IN HIS OR HER RIGHT MIND WOULD REQUEST A HEALING . . .

Some people who read this information will find the idea of restoring cause and effect abhorrent. In fact, the human aspect of each person rejects anything that causes it to change or to sacrifice its own goals. The human aspect lives only for the short run. However, there is actually no short run. There is only the long road of spiritual evolution that eventually must be traveled by everyone.

The human aspect of any person is not concerned with whether that person is moving spiritually or not. It does not care if the person will be coming back into incarnation again, repeating the same going-nowhere ideas and patterns that he or she has had in this lifetime. The human aspect only cares about fulfilling its own temporary goals and desires, which is why it is so difficult for the Brotherhood to reach humanity at this time.

If you want a healing to be transmitted to you, you can request one by writing to Gentle Wind, or calling during the hours listed at the end of this chapter. Understand, however, that you will begin an irreversible process of continuous failure of your human goals and ideas until the spiritual aspect of you—your own Monad—can regain its rightful control over your life.

If you are not prepared to face the failure of your own human goals, you should not request this healing. You should wait until you are convinced that what your human aspect wants to do with your life will not bring you the satisfaction you are seeking. Unfortunately, most people do not make this discovery until they are too old to do anything about it. Some people even die and return to the Inner World without being completely convinced that what they did with their lives was a useless waste. Some who know clearly that their lives have been wasted are too damaged and depleted to do anything about it even in the Inner World, so they simply come right back into physical incarnation and repeat the same useless lives.

WHO DO YOU PEOPLE THINK YOU ARE?

Some "spiritual types" who have just read this book, particularly this chapter, are now outraged by what they have read. We would first remind those readers that We warned them at the beginning of this book not to read any further unless they were prepared to change something about themselves. Not only are they still going the wrong way with their lives, but now they are completely aware that they are doing so. It is painful enough to be wasting your life on human goals and objectives, but to know you are doing so is unbearable. In order to be able to continue in the same direction, these people must now waste more of their precious spiritual resources in attempting to discredit this book.

What these "spiritual types" are really saying is, "Who does the Logos think He is?" The Logos is actually far too advanced spiritually, however, to either think about who He is or to "be" anybody. This healing project is being conducted through the office of the Logos Who has the help and assistance of His teachers' teachers. It is a project that by its nature is a confrontation to people who are not doing what they came here to do. The real problem for these people, then, is not who anyone thinks anyone else is. Spiritual types who are not doing what they came here to do can only remain content with themselves as long as they are surrounded with other spiritual types who are not doing what they came here to do. The more irate a person is about what he or she has read in this book, the further off course that person is likely to be. The more people try to discredit this book, the more painful being off course will become.

WHAT CAN I DO?

You can receive a transmitted healing by calling or writing to Gentle Wind and requesting that this healing be sent to you. If you notice any positive results from this healing, you can tell other people about what you know. The results are actually positive for everyone, but only people who have imagination are able to perceive what is really happening to them. People without any imagination forget about their transmitted healings, even though they are often the ones with the most obvious and profound changes in their lives. There is nothing you can do to acquire imagination. You either have it or you do not.

You can also read the books suggested at the end of this section. These books should be read in the spirit in which they were written. They are meant to nurture the mind. Much of the damage that has been done to people has occurred in school, during the education process. The next book in this series will help to explain why and how education has destroyed the human consciousness, and how this has made evolution even more impossible.

The regeneration and recovery process requires nurturing the mind. These books were not written to be memorized, nor were they written to cause spiritual growth. They were written to quiet and calm the human mind. The best way to read them is to choose the book that feels right and open it to any page. Read until you feel like stopping, which might be after only a few sentences or a page. Then put the book down and do not read any more that day.

To obtain further information about these healings or to request the healing for yourself and any members of your family, write to Gentle Wind, or call between 9:00 A.M. and 7:00 P.M., seven days a week.

Gentle Wind Retreat
P.O. Box 184
Surry, Maine 04684

In Maine: (207) 374-5478

Outside of Maine:
1-800-255-5199

Book List

The following books are published by the Agni Yoga Society, 319 West 107th Street, New York, New York 10025:

New Era Community, 1926

Agni Yoga, 1929

Infinity, 1930

Hierarchy, 1931

Heart, 1932

Fiery World, 1933

Fiery World II, 1934

Fiery World III, 1935

Aum, 1936

Mother of the World, 1956

The following books are published by DeVorss and Company, Publishers, P.O. Box 550, Marina del Rey, California 90294:

The Way Out

The Way to the Kingdom

The Impersonal Life

Brotherhood

From Gentle Wind Retreat, P.O. Box 184, Surry, Maine 04684, or Bergin & Garvey Publishers, Inc. 670 Amherst Road, South Hadley, Massachusetts 01075:

The Psychology of Spiritual Growth, published in 1987 by Bergin & Garvey Publishers.

Modern Education: One Size Fits All, to be published in 1988 by Bergin & Garvey Publishers.